POLITICS IN LATIN AMERICA
A HOOVER INSTITUTION SERIES

General Editor, **Robert Wesson**

Copublished with Hoover Institution Press,
Stanford University, Stanford, California

THE MEXICAN RULING PARTY
Stability and Authority

Dale Story

POLITICS IN LATIN AMERICA, A Hoover Institution Series

New York
Westport, Connecticut
London

Library of Congress Cataloging-in-Publication Data

Story, Dale, 1950–
The Mexican ruling party.

(Politics in Latin America)
Bibliography: p.
Includes index.
1. Partido Revolucionario Institucional—History.
2. Mexico—Politics and government.   I. Title.
II. Series.
JL1298.R45S86   1986   324.272'05   86-22690
ISBN 0-275-92127-1 (alk. paper)

*The Hoover Institution on War, Revolution and Peace, founded at
Stanford University in 1919 by the late President Herbert Hoover
is an interdisciplinary research center for advanced study on
domestic and international affairs in the twentieth century. The
views expressed in its publications are entirely those of the
authors and do not reflect the views of the staff, officers, or
Board of Overseers of the Hoover Institution.*

Library of Congress Catalog Card Number: 86-22690
ISBN: 0-275-92127-1

First published in 1986 by Praeger Publishers

Praeger Publishers, 521 Fifth Avenue, New York, NY 10175
A Division of Greenwood Press, Inc.

Printed in the United States of America

∞

The paper used in this book complies with the
Permanent Paper Standard issued by the National
Information Standards Organization (Z39.48-1984).

10 9 8 7 6 5 4 3 2 1

To Alejandro and Arian

Contents

List of Illustrations

TABLES

Preface

Most research on Mexico adopts one of two differing points of view. A positive bias stresses viewing Mexico relative to other authoritarian regimes in Latin America, and a negative bias emphasizes comparing Mexico to our perception of U.S. standards or to our own preferences of what Mexico ought to be. The former perspective concludes that Mexico has achieved remarkable political stability, an envious economic record, and a reasonably free and open political system. The latter viewpoint finds that the Mexican Revolution is a myth, that stability has been maintained only through a corporatist system, and that economic growth is heavily dependent upon external forces and is not self-sustaining. Neither side is wrong. But the differing points of comparison lead to seeing the cup as either half-full or half-empty.

Though I will have many critical points to make, this book definitely falls under the positive bias—viewing the Mexican cup as half-full compared to many of its Latin American neighbors. The word "relative" is probably overworked in these chapters. It refers to Mexico's authoritarianism as benign, some of its interest groups as autonomous, its economic growth as a miracle, and its political system as stable—all relative to the standards of the region. The faults and weaknesses of the Mexican one-party system are not to be excused, nor are the miserable standards of living under which most Mexicans suffer. But Mexico nonetheless provides an economic and political model that most Latin American nations would be quite satisfied to emulate.

1

Introduction

Mexico is most often described by political scientists as a one-party authoritarian state. A major U.S. newspaper referred to Mexico as the "modern world's most long-lived example of a one-party state."[1] Power is centralized in the hands of a virtually omnipotent president, who is always the candidate of the dominant or ruling party—the Institutional Revolutionary Party (Partido Revolucionario Institucional, or PRI). Since its formation in 1929, the PRI has not lost a presidential election and has lost very few contests for other national, state, and local positions.

The significance of the PRI is exemplified in a concrete fashion by the party's visual symbols that are conspicuous throughout Mexico. After all, it is the "party of the Revolution." Its colors (green and red) are the national colors. Its candidates frequently evoke the names of Juárez, Madero, Zapata, Carranza, and others as if the present-day PRI leaders were the political descendants of the popular founders of the Mexican state. During campaigns PRI slogans and signs dominate the landscape, often covering whole sides of large hotels on the major avenues of Mexico City. In comparison, the advertisements for the opposition parties are confined to small billboards on side streets or to posters (that are quickly defaced) pasted to vacant buildings or crumbling walls.

As evidence of the power of the PRI to penetrate Mexican society, stories abound of the degree to which an individual's livelihood, security, and allegiance are tied to the ruling party. Ambitious politicians know that the path to electoral power is monopolized by the PRI and that the opposition parties offer no genuine opportunities for rising to influential positions. Even among the lower classes the hope for a better life usually centers around the PRI. One example can serve as an illustration. The son of a poor maid in Mexico City travels to southern

Mexico in search of a job and, through the oil workers union (a PRI affiliate), gains employment in the oil fields. He wires the majority of his wages in his mother in Mexico City. Yet his mother cannot receive the money at the telegram office without sufficient identification. Having her employer, a wealthy realtor, accompany her and vouch for her is not deemed sufficient by the authorities, but they do promise to release the money to her if she will acquire an identification card from the PRI. The maid does not object, since she always votes for the PRI (despite the existence of parties that some argue better represent her class interests), often attends their rallies, and is reinspired every six years by the myth of the revolution as manifested in the presidential inaugural parade. Thus, she has been socialized to remain loyal to the PRI and even depends upon the official party for her son's job and for her identification necessary to receive his money by wire. Though the details of this situation may be unique, the extensive degree to which the PRI permeates the lives of this woman and her son is not an unusual occurrence.

Thus, Mexico may appear to be the prototype of a one-party authoritarian state. Yet this classification, when viewed more specifically and comparatively, may be a serious oversimplification. The PRI obviously differs in many respects from the official party in Cuba, which is much more ideological and domineering than the Mexican party. And Mexico's brand of authoritarianism is much less harsh than that practiced by many Southern Cone countries, such as Chile under Pinochet, Brazil in the late-1960s, or Argentina in the late-1970s. Some analysts refer to the Mexican variant as "benign authoritarianism." Whatever the label, scholars agree that the Mexican system is unique—a multifaceted hybrid of several characteristics.

Despite differences regarding the political classification of the Mexican system, all analysts recognize two outstanding achievements of modern Mexico: (1) remarkable and consistent political stability, in conjunction with (2) economic growth in the postwar period often characterized as an "economic miracle." In a region not incorrectly associated with coups and other forms of political violence, Mexico is one of the few Latin American nations enjoying decades of political stability. The military has not intervened in politics, eight successful and peaceful transitions of presidential power have occurred over six decades, and examples of state violence against citizens or civilian insurrection are the exception rather than the rule.

Mexico has also achieved an economic record almost unrivaled in the region. In the four decades since 1940, Mexico has enjoyed an average annual growth rate in Gross Domestic Product (GDP) of over 6 percent, and until recently inflation has consistently remained below 5 percent annually. In the mid-1970s Mexico became a net exporter of petroleum for the first time since the 1920s, and in a few years emerged as one of the world's major suppliers of hydrocarbons. Yet the Mexican economy is not a typical export-oriented situation completely vulnerable to the market fluctuations of a particular primary product. In fact, Mexico is credited with being one of the newly industrialized countries (or NICs) along with the likes of Taiwan, Hong Kong, Singapore, and South Korea. Mexico has built a strong industrial base in the postwar period. By 1980 the industrial sector accounted for 37 percent of the GDP and manufactured goods represented 39 percent of all exports.[2]

Of course, the postwar political stability and economic growth in Mexico have not occurred without serious problems and trade-offs. The most recent threats to political calm include the 1968 student-worker demonstrations and killing of several hundred peaceful demonstrators on October 2, 1968 (the so-called Tlatelolco Massacre), uneasy presidential transitions in 1976 and 1982 marked by economic instability and rumors of a military coup, and predictions of growing social unrest in the 1980s associated with the economic austerity program adopted after the debt crisis of 1981. In regard to the postwar economic miracle, the most significant trade-off has been in the area of income distribution. Though figures on income distribution are far from exact, most analysts agree that Mexico has among the most inequitable patterns of income distribution in Latin America.[3] Furthermore, the economic success story seemed to have reached its limits in the 1980s. The petroleum boom of the late-1970s had provided a temporary respite, but the economic crisis of 1982 brought 100 percent inflation, negative real economic growth, and the postponement of debt payments. Despite these caveats, the overall political stability and economic progress of postwar Mexico are widely recognized as major accomplishments by almost all analysts of the Mexican scene.

Scholarly agreement breaks down, however, on classifying the Mexican political system. At least four different interpretations can be identified: (1) the democratic, pluralist perspective; (2) the thesis of limited state autonomy; (3) the authoritarian framework; and (4) the authoritarian variant stressing the autonomy of certain societal groups. Certainly, the distinctions are not mutually exclusive but rather involve the positioning of the Mexican state on a continuum ranging between the ideal-types of democracy and authoritarianism. No one argues that Mexico is a perfect example of either extreme. But obvious and substantial differences do exist regarding exactly where Mexico lies on this political spectrum.

Emphasizing that democracy is preferable to authoritarianism, the most optimistic viewpoints stress the existence of many democratic traits in Mexico and claim that the movement toward democracy there is genuine and irreversible. One North American political scientist finds "evidence of a great deal of positive accomplishment in the struggle to establish working democracy in Mexico."[4] A noted Mexican scholar concludes that all analyses of Mexican development lead to the same, inescapable conclusion—the development of "capitalist democracy."[5] The U.S. State Department describes Mexico as a "presidential-legislative democracy" and stresses that voter participation has increased from 59 percent in 1964 (over 9 million votes) to 75 percent in 1982 (over 22 million votes).[6]

These optimistic interpretations focus on the constitutional trappings of democracy that do exist on the surface in Mexico: popular sovereignty, political equality, popular consultation, and majority rule with protections for minority rights. Contested elections occur, and relatively high rates of voluntary voter participation are consistently achieved. Universal suffrage exists, and the principle of one person–one vote is professed. Various political parties and interest groups operate openly. Often vitriolic demonstrations by opposition groups serve as examples of freedom of association and of expression. Censorship is not overtly obvious. The concept of no reelection insures a regular turnover in elected officials. Minority groups are assured some legislative representation through a system of proportional representation. In sum, many of the major aspects of a democratic system nominally exist in Mexico.

However, some obvious exceptions to the democratic mode in Mexico can be cited. Without yet examining the actual degree of political freedom or the issue of whether the opposition parties are truly independent, a telling fact is that the opposition has never won a presidential election (the maximum opposition vote in a presidential election was 24 percent in 1982). Also, the opposition has never achieved a majority in the national legislature (the maximum opposition vote in elections for the Chamber of Deputies was 30 percent scattered among eight parties in 1979). The pattern of allowing only token opposition seems clear.

The conceptualization of Mexico as a pluralist state is especially difficult to accept. Philippe C. Schmitter defines pluralism as:

> a system of interest representation in which the constituent units are organized into an unspecified number of multiple, voluntary, competitive, nonhierarchically ordered and self-determined (as to type or scope of interest) categories which are not specially licensed, recognized, subsidized, created or otherwise controlled in leadership selection or interest articulation by the state and which do not exercise a monopoly of representational activity within their respective categories.[7]

Contrary to this conceptualization, most interest groups in Mexico (especially those for labor and peasants) are characterized by compulsory membership, lack of competition, hierarchical relationships, and little or no autonomy from the state. All the major interest groups except those of the private sector are officially incorporated into the PRI, and even the business groups are granted a monopoly of representation by the state. The Mexican interest group system comes much closer to Schmitter's definition of corporatism: "singular, compulsory, noncompetitive, hierarchically ordered and functionally differentiated categories, recognized or licensed (if not created) by the state."[8]

A second view of the Mexican political system stresses the notion of limited state autonomy.[9] This interpretation claims that the autonomy of the state is severely constrained by powerful economic elites and by their commitment to promote private capital accumulation. State interests are said to be identified with and really controlled by the economic power of private capital. The role of the state in promoting private capital expansion and "dependent capitalist development" is often cited as a manifestation of the capitalist dominance over the Mexican state. The congruence of interests of economic and political elites and their formal and informal linkages are seen as another example of this phenomenon. Indeed, the ties of political leaders with the private sector have a long history in Mexico, beginning with such "entrepreneurs turned revolutionaries" as Francisco Madero, Venustiano Carranza, and Aarón Sáenz. A few examples of close business-state relations in the postwar period include industrialist and former president Miguel Alemán, wealthy investor and former major of Mexico City Carlos Hank González, and adviser to industrial associations and powerful PRI leader Jesús Reyes Heroles.

The essence of the limited state automony argument is that the state is dominated by influential capitalist interests. Certainly, the private sector and the state in Mexico share many concerns, and the entrepreneurial class is an extremely powerful political actor. Since the inception of the one-party state in the late-1920s, public policy has heavily favored the interests of economic elites and the goal of capital accumulation. However, the state has not simply been a tool of the private sector. As will be seen later, the state frequently balances policies benefiting one segment of the population with decisions that reward a different segment. Though the state and private sector do coalesce as an "alliance for profits" on some issues, the state reserves the autonomy to alter or break this alliance through redistributive decisions such as nationalizations, agrarian reform, or expanded state regulation. Certainly, the entrepreneurial class was not dictating policy to the political elite when Cárdenas expropriated the land and nationalized the oil companies and railroads in the 1930s, when López Mateos purchased control of various foreign companies and implemented the profit-sharing plan in the early-1960s, when Echeverría greatly expanded the economic role of the state and strongly criticized the Monterrey industrialists in the 1970s, or most recently when López Portillo adopted exchange controls and nationalized the banks in 1982. This shifting of allegiances by the state has been a critical factor in maintaining the political stability of Mexico. If the Mexican government truly was a captive of the private sector, the one-party state might not have survived.

Probably the most widely accepted interpretation of the Mexican state emphasizes the authoritarian framework, which was initially established by Juan J. Linz in examining Spain and later applied to Mexico by Susan Kaufman Purcell.[10] The concept of authoritarianism was first stressed in the 1960s as an important alterative to the traditional dichotomy in regime classification between democracy and totalitarianism. This regime type has been particularly relevant to Latin America since the mid-1960s. Authoritarianism has usually been described as incorporating three characteristics distinct from those of democratic or totalitarian systems: limited political pluralism, low subject mobilization, and hierarchical ordering of relationships. Limited pluralism (akin to Schmitter's definition of corporatism) denotes that interest groups are dependent upon and controlled by the regime and that the ideology and actions of the groups serve the interests of the regime rather than those of their membership. In situations of low subject mobilization, citizens are mobilized only to support the state and only in temporary cases. In other words, political participation is at very low levels. Hierarchical ordering of relationships infers centralized and patronal leadership in the political arena. The ruling elites grant benefits to select groups or leaders who then defer to the regime and offer support. The patronal subordination and co-optation of inferiors continues down the political hierarchy. The dominant trend among social scientists in recent years has been to conclude that Mexico incorporates most of these characteristics of an authoritarian state.[11]

The final view of the Mexican state, and that emphasized in this book, recognizes the relevance of the broad label of authoritarianism to Mexico but stresses that Mexico represents an important and somewhat more benign variant of the authoritarian state. Political repression is neither as extensive nor as overt as in many other authoritarian Latin American states. The "carrot" is preferred to the "stick," and control is achieved through subtle political strategies emphasizing co-optation and mollification.[12] Finally, various political groups are recognized as exercising considerable autonomy from the state. In reevaluating the applicability of the authoritarian label to Mexico, several analysts have posited the existence of relative autonomy from the Mexican state on the part of certain political segments and have emphasized a policy process characterized by bargaining among elite groups with different interests.[13]

The relationship between the private sector and the state in Mexico provides one of the best examples of the autonomy of interest groups. Most significantly, all business organizations are officially independent of the governing party. While the PRI dominates other actors by incorporating labor, the peasantry, and the middle class (especially government employees) within the structure of the party, entrepreneurial groups have remained outside the party's umbrella. Several authors have noted that the private sector is quite content with its position outside the PRI since business groups can realize their objectives through other channels while escaping the rigors of party discipline.[14]

Political repression certainly exists in Mexico. Human rights groups have charged that at least 500 political dissidents have disappeared over recent years.[15] Allegations of torture, arbitrary arrests, and even politically motivated killings are frequently made. The media is greatly influenced by the economic impact of government advertising and government control of the newsprint. Yet the degree to which basic human liberties are violated in Mexico is not as great as in most authoritarian Latin American states.

Freedom House is the only human rights group that compares the records of all countries, and its data suggest that Mexico is one of the "freest" of the authoritarian states in Latin America. Freedom House ranks all countries on a scale from 1 to 7 according to their guarantees for political rights and for civil liberties (1 being most free and 7 being least free). It also classifies governments in three categories: free, partly free, and not free. Of the twenty Latin American republics that gained their independence by the first decade of this century, Freedom House classified nine as "free" in 1984 (see Table 1). Yet of the remaining eleven "partly free" or "not free" countries, nine rank worse than Mexico on the measures of political rights and civil liberties.[16] And in 1984 the U.S. State Department was optimistic about improvements in the Mexican human rights record. It concluded its 1983 annual report on human rights in Mexico by saying that "the trend of Mexican compliance with generally-accepted standards of respect for human rights is positive."[17]

In focusing on the ruling party in Mexico, this book clearly takes sides in the scholarly debate over the appropriate typology for the Mexican political system: the authoritarian variant in which political repression is not overt and some important groups enjoy relative autonomy from the state. Thus, in addition to the common themes of political stability and economic growth in Mexico, this book adds a third: that these outcomes are at least partly due to the dominant single party which has helped establish a "benignly authoritarian" state. The role of the ruling party and its impact on the political system will be analyzed by first examining the historical evolution of the PRI and the so-called pendulum effect before turning to the electoral successes of the Party (including the role of opposition parties), the internal structure and workings of the Party and its incorporation of major interest groups, and the relationship between the PRI and political elites.

Finally, the book concludes by reviewing the two major challenges

Table 1 Comparative Measures of Freedom, 1985[a]

	Political Rights	Civil Liberties	Status of Freedom[b]
1. Costa Rica	1	1	F
2. Venezuela	1	2	F
3. Dominican Republic	1	3	F
4. Ecuador	2	2	F
5. Peru	2	3	F
6. Colombia	2	3	F
7. Bolivia	2	3	F
8. Argentina	2	2	F
9. Honduras	2	3	F
10. Brazil	3	3	PF
11. Mexico	3	4	PF
12. Panama	4	3	PF
13. El Salvador	3	5	PF
14. Uruguay	5	4	PF
15. Paraguay	5	5	PF
16. Nicaragua	5	5	PF
17. Chile	6	5	PF
18. Guatemala	5	6	PF
19. Cuba	6	6	NF
20. Haiti	7	6	NF

Source: Raymond D. Gastil, "The Comparative Survey of Freedom 1985," *Freedom at Issue*, no. 82 (January–February 1985); 8–9.

[a] As of January 1985.
[b] F = free; PF = partly free; and NF = not free. See source for definitions and methodology.

presently facing the PRI: the declining linkages between the party and the true centers of political power in Mexico (the president of the Republic and his cabinet) and the apparent deterioration in popular support for the PRI in recent years. The key decision-makers, at least within the last two decades, have come increasingly from more technical and bureaucratic backgrounds with less political (specifically electoral) experience and substantially fewer ties to the party. Though arguments that the PRI is becoming politically irrelevant are exaggerations, the traditional dominance of the ruling party is being seriously tested on two fronts: (1) electoral opposition, especially from the right of the political spectrum; and (2) autonomous decision-making by a new technocratic class within the executive branch.

2

Birth of the Ruling Party

In his comparative study of party systems in Latin America, Ronald H. McDonald identified six countries as having "single-party dominant systems" in 1971: Mexico, Nicaragua, El Salvador, Cuba, Haiti, and Paraguay.[1] Of these six, Mexico is the prototype of a state in which the official party is a central figure in the political process. On the other extreme, Haiti is the case in which the party was irrelevant—largely an appendage of the personal power of the "President-for-life," Jean-Claude Duvalier. The parties in Cuba and Paraguay also are secondary to other political institutions or actors. And since events of the late-1970s, the party systems of Nicaragua and El Salvador have been evolving in somewhat different directions. Thus, Mexico remains the best example of a one-party state with a relevant and powerful single party that is not subordinate to either the army, a charismatic leader, powerful interest groups, or an ideological cadre. In Mexico the PRI truly dominates the electoral scene, and is a key instrument buttressing the administrative elite headed by the president. Therefore, an understanding of contemporary Mexican politics requires that we begin with a basic overview of the history of the ruling party.

The PRI was not born officially until after the Mexican Revolution, but the Liberal-Conservative battles of the nineteenth century and especially the harsh repression of the regime of Porfirio Díaz (1876–1910) had a profound impact on the revolutionary leaders who established the roots of the ruling party. And even if only indirectly, prerevolutionary individuals like Juárez, Ocampo, Lerdo, the Flores Magón brothers, and General Díaz himself had a role in the shaping of the PRI. Thus, we begin with a discussion of the events leading up to the Revolution of 1910.

NINETEENTH-CENTURY PRECURSORS

Unlike some of the other more advanced Latin American nations (especially Argentina and Chile), Mexico did not develop strong, institutionalized political parties in the nineteenth century. As was the case in most of the region, Mexican politics in the 1800s were marked by political struggles between the Conservatives and the Liberals. However, in Mexico these were not strongly organized political parties— rather they were loose amalgams coalesced around the power base of various *caudillos*.

Though both groups were elitist, their ideological differences were profound. The Liberals of Mexico were anticlerics who sought to curb the powers and privileges of the traditional power centers of the church and the military. They supported democratic reforms, believed in a federal form of government (more power to the provinces), and followed laissez-faire economic policies. On the other hand, the Conservatives received the support of the Church, the military, and traditional landed interests (the *hacendados*). They preferred more protectionism, less political liberty, and a centralist form of government (power still concentrated in Mexico City). Despite these distinctions, neither party overcame its self-serving and narrow political base in order to survive as a modern political party. Their primary purpose was to provide the philosophical underpinnings for ambitious political leaders.

As the political parties of the day did not establish the strong roots for a modern party system in Mexico, neither did they produce any semblance of political stability until well into the second half of the nineteenth century. From the time of political independence in 1821 until the end of the Three Years War in 1860, Mexico saw at least 50 presidencies, 35 being led by army officers. Throughout these four decades, the Liberals and Conservatives preferred to resolve their differences through armed struggle rather than peaceful politics. Of course, the lack of stability at this time was not due solely to the failure of the political parties. Mexico was also plagued with tremendous economic problems (largely owing to a lack of resources) such as massive internal deficits and external debts. The latter gave cause for various foreign interventions (the 1838 war with France and the 1861 occupation by Spain, France, and England) which further diminished domestic political stability.

The Liberals (or Federalists, as they were sometimes labeled) were the strongest force in the first decade after independence; and the 1824 constitution is usually described as a liberal document, since the major accomplishment was the establishment of a federal republic in Mexico. However, the Conservatives (or Centralists) also persevered on a number of key points: the Catholic Church retained its monopoly position over spiritual matters, the clergy and the military were afforded virtual immunity from civil law, and the office of the presidency was granted strong powers. And with the election of General Antonio López de Santa Anna Pérez de Lebrón in 1833 the Conservatives officially assumed the leadership position in a persistently volatile political system.

Santa Anna was the dominant political force over the next twenty years, though he was not a very popular or successful leader. This period has been described as "constantly teeter[ing] between simple chaos and unmitigated anarchy" and Santa Anna as "Mexico's most despised, traitorous, duplicitous native son."[2] Prior to first coming to power in 1833 (he was president on eleven different occasions), he was noted as a defender of liberal causes. However, in office he was the consummate conservative. He abolished the previous, federalist constitution and promulgated the constitution of 1836, which was a centralist and aristocratic document. The liberal outcry together with the growing resentments of the citizens of the northern province of Texas eventually provoked the disastrous war with the United States in 1846, in which Santa Anna was held responsible for losing about half of Mexico's territory. Through the 1848 Treaty of Guadalupe Hidalgo ending the war, the former Mexican states of Texas, New Mexico, and California were sold to the United States for just over $18 million. In 1853 Santa Anna sold another chunk of Mexican territory (present-day southern Arizona and New Mexico) for another $10 million (the so-called Gadsden Purchase).

The Liberals regrouped to oust Santa Anna for the last time in the 1855 Revolution of Ayutla. A new period of Mexican history—known as *La Reforma*—was initiated. A new generation of secular and antimilitarist intellectuals with a strong social consciousness and profound nationalistic spirit came to the forefront of Mexican politics. Their philosophical commitments and political successes were embodied in leaders like Melchor Ocampo—son of a *hacendado*; avid reader of Proudhon, Voltaire, and Rousseau; and former governor of Michoacán—and Benito Juárez—full-blooded Zapotec Indian and former governor of Oaxaca. These and other new liberal leaders promptly began "The Reform" with two new laws. The *Ley Juárez* of 1855 ended the exemptions from civil jurisdiction that clerics and soldiers had enjoyed; and the *Ley Lerdo* of 1856 mandated that all "corporate bodies" (i.e., the Church) divest themselves of all property not used in daily, religious functions (i.e., the church's massive landholdings). The Constitution of 1857 endorsed federalism and political liberties, incorporating the *Ley Juárez* and the *Ley Lerdo*, and rejecting the special privileges previously accorded to the political and economic elites.

Juárez began his first presidential term in 1860, but his tenure was abruptly interrupted by the French occupation of 1862. The French emperor, Napoleon III, decided to install the Austrian archduke Ferdinand Maximilian of Hapsburg as the newly designated emperor of Mexico. Though Mexico Conservatives were consulted and were supportive (especially since Juárez was forced to evacuate Mexico City), the new emperor was a Mason and possessed some liberal leanings. He refused to reestablish Catholicism as the monopoly religion, and he rejected pressures to return church lands. Still, he was no ally of the Mexican Liberals who persisted in their armed struggle to oust the foreign monarchy.

In the face of international pressure, Napoleon decided to withdraw French troops in 1866. Maximilian soon fell from power and was executed in May of 1867. Juárez then returned to power in 1867 and decided to seek another presidential term in 1871. Though he won the presidency in 1871, his candidacy split the liberal ranks. General Porfirio Díaz, a former supporter of Juárez in the campaign against the French, was one of the losers in that election of 1871. After his electoral defeat, Díaz suffered a military defeat in his unsuccessful revolution to overthrow Juárez. Evoking an image that was to haunt him later, Díaz based his revolt on the slogan of "no reelection."

The death of Juárez in 1872 brought another liberal, Sebastián Lerdo de Tejada (brother of the author of the *Ley Lerdo*), to the presidency. Like Juárez before him, Lerdo attempted to succeed himself in 1876. And once again Porfirio Díaz revolted under the banner of "no reelection." However, on this occasion Díaz succeeded. As Lerdo fled to the United States, Díaz occupied Mexico City on November 21, 1876—a date that some commentators mark as the beginning of modern Mexico.

The initiation of a modern Mexico under Díaz was certainly obvious in an economic sense. Guided by the policies of a group of Mexican followers of French positivism (called *científicos*), the economy did begin to develop rapidly. The *científicos* stressed order, rationality, and economic liberalism. Drawing heavily upon European influences (the best example being José Limantour, son of a Frenchman and secretary of the treasury under Díaz), the *científicos* denigrated the role of the indigenous peoples who were perceived to be "irrational." Foreign investment, particularly British and U.S., was encouraged and soon took command of key sectors. By the end of the *Porfiriato* (the reign of Porfirio Díaz from 1876 to 1910, which was interrupted only briefly between 1880 and 1884), foreign investment was reported to account for fully one-half of the total wealth in Mexico.[3] Probably the greatest accomplishment of foreign capital was the construction of the railways, which greatly expanded the domestic market and also aided the exportation of primary products. Exports, particularly gold and silver, increased 500 percent. Under the 1884 Mining Law and the 1901 Petroleum Law, which gave subsoil rights to surface owners (usually foreign investors), much of the investment in the extractive industries came from abroad. Even the industrial sector progressed, as exemplified by the establishment of Mexico's first iron and steel plant, the Compañía Fundidora de Fierro y Acero de Monterrey. One private report in 1883 claimed some 3,000 industrial establishments in existence at that time, and an official survey shows a total of 6,234 industrial establishments in 1902.[4]

Much of this economic progress was directly attributable to the political stabiilty of the *Porfiriato*—really the first period of political order "enjoyed" by an independent Mexico. Though Díaz was a product of the liberal movement in Mexico, he did not emphasize liberal democratic philosophies once in office. At best he was neutral on the issue of the church. And, most significantly, after 1880 he defied his own dogma of no reelection and showed no inclinations toward political democracy. The stability of that era was achieved through the firm dictatorial control of Porfirio Díaz, who created a very centralized government that concentrated political and economic power in the hands of an aristocratic elite. In sum, his rule was a brutal military dictatorship in which the dreaded *rurales* enforced order in the countryside through fear and intimidation.

THE REVOLUTION

Until 1910 the Liberals and the Conservatives were the only political parties that Mexico had known, and these could only be loosely construed as parties. Though their ideology was reasonably well developed, their organization was very weak and decentralized. Two factors had worked against the emergence of strong parties in Mexico during the *Porfiriato* (and even during the Revolutionary period). In the first place, the regional power of local *caudillos* had undermined all attempts to establish a strong national base for a political party. Second, neither an independent entrepreneurial class nor a significant middle class had emerged. Thus, the roots for a mass-based, reformist party (similar to the Radicals in Argentina) were lacking in Mexico.

Although no well-established parties existed to lead the opposition, as early as 1895 various individual Liberals did begin to present intellectual arguments against the dictatorial rule of Díaz. The arrest in 1900 of the Flores Magón brothers, who were probably the most influential opposition leaders at that time was one of the first measures catalyzing the adversaries of the *Porfiriato*. This action prompted many Liberals, including Francisco Madero (the son of a wealthy *hacendado* in Coahuila), to contribute to the cause of the opposition.

From their exile in the United States in the summer of 1906 the Flores Magón brothers published their Liberal Plan, which updated typical nineteenth-century doctrine (political freedoms and secularization) with a discussion of uniquely twentieth-century social and economic issues (ranging from eight-hour workdays to the prohibition of child labor). Other liberal sympathizers were leading crucial labor strikes in Mexico: the 1906 strike at the Cananea copper mine in Sonora, the worker uprising at the textile mills in Rio Blanco in 1907, and the railroad strike in 1908. Some analysts suggest that these labor strikes were the first manifestations of the Revolution, but the most powerful catalyst to the opposition came in 1908.[5]

In an interview with the U.S. journalist James Creelman in early 1908, Díaz made the astounding announcement that he did not plan to seek reelection in the 1910 presidential election. The slogan of "no reelection" had been utilized first in 1871 by Díaz himself, and now he was resurrecting that political doctrine. The difference in 1908 was that the cry of "no reelection" was now the rallying point of the opposition. This pronouncement by Díaz led to much political activity, mostly from the Liberals, in the following two years. The most significant event was the publication of a book by Francisco Madero (*La sucesión presidencial en 1910*), which urged the formation of a new party under the banner of "no reelection." The unpredictable Díaz decided to run after all, and his candidacy along with Madero's book contributed to the ascendancy of the anti-reelectionist cause. The first revolutionary party was born in April of 1910 when a convention of *anti-reelectionistas* nominated Madero for president.

Díaz responded to the new party by jailing Madero and securing his own reelection in the fraudulent election of June 21, 1910. However, Madero escaped from his imprisonment in San Luis Potosí and fled to the United States. In October from San Antonio, Texas, Madero issued his famous *Plan de San Luis Potosí*, in which he criticized the election of Díaz as illegal and called for a revolution to begin on November 20. The opposition in Mexico, led primarily by old-line Liberals and newer members of the anti-reelectionist movement, began to prepare for the armed struggle to overthrow the Díaz dictatorship.

Even Madero was surprised by the overwhelming reaction to his call for a revolution. Widespread disenchantment with the three previous decades of repression sparked an outpouring of armed, though spontaneous and somewhat disorganized, opposition to Díaz. The Revolution had begun and would engulf Mexico for the next decade.

The Mexican Revolution, directed against the ruling coalition of foreign interests and the agro-mining export elites, was fought by a variety of previously dispossessed groups, with the most well-known probably being the Mexican peasantry. In addition to the role of the peasantry, an important component in the Revolution was the struggle between sectoral elites.[6] An aspiring political and economic elite was as crucial to the revolutionary cause as were the rural masses. Also, the incipient industrial sector, both entrepreneurs and labor, supported the Revolution and benefited from it.

The military struggle in its initial stage was led by Pascual Orozco and his lieutenant Pancho Villa, who battled the Díaz troops in the north. Within months the government forces had suffered a major defeat at Ciudad Juárez, and federal soldiers began to defect in droves. With his political and military support crumbling, Díaz resigned on May 25, 1911.

Despite its sudden success, or possibly because of it, the revolutionary coalition still was not united. The cleavages in the dominant coalition that were to linger into the 1920s were typical of the failed attempts in the nineteenth century to create strong political parties or even to maintain a well-organized political movement. At the time of the overthrow of Díaz, the disputes among the new leaders were many. First, military leaders like Orozco (a mule skinner from Chihuahua) quarreled with the political leadership under Madero. The more radical politicians were pitted against the moderates. More divisions were soon to follow. In the state of Morelos, Emiliano Zapata and his peasant followers took up arms against Madero. Yet, in the midst of all these disputes, Madero won the presidency in new elections on October 1, 1911.

Commenting on the political instability facing Mexico at that time, on his way to exile Díaz reportedly remarked: "Madero has unleashed a tiger. Now let's see if he can control it."[7] Events soon proved that Madero could not control the disparate elements of the Revolution. The new president was an idealist—ill-suited for administering the affairs of a nation, especially one in turmoil. His inability to provide new direction for Mexico disappointed even his supporters. The Liberals were distraught with Madero's performance, particularly the slow pace of reforms. The *zapatistas* lamented the lack of agrarian reform and were the first to declare themselves in revolt against the new regime in November of 1911 (shortly after Madero had tried to demobilize the peasant army of Zapata). Representing numerous other strains of disaffection, three separate revolts soon broke out in the north and still another in Veracruz. The end to the Madero presidency finally came in February 1913.

Madero was overthrown by the forces of counterrevolution. A military revolt was initiated by those sympathetic to the *Porfiriato*, and after ten days of very bitter fighting General Victoriano Huerta, who was Madero's chief commander (but a former *porfirista* general as well) switched sides to join the counterrevolution. With the help of Huerta and the complicity of the U.S. ambassador, Madero was removed from office, arrested, and murdered by his guards while he was being transferred to another prison.

General Huerta had many enemies, and his strong-armed rule was unable to restore the political order of the *Porfiriato*. One of his most important opponents was the governor of Coahuila and Madero supporter, Venustiano Carranza, who was soon named the "First Chief" of the Constitutionalist Army established to overthrow Huerta. Pancho Villa and Alvaro Obregón were crucial military allies of Carranza in the north, and Zapata continued his armed struggle for land in the south. Another crucial antagonist was U.S. president, Woodrow Wilson, who was openly hostile to Huerta and was willing to use U.S. influence to assist the Constitutionalists under Carranza. Wilson saw Carranza as better representing the values of moderation and democracy. When U.S. sailors were arrested in the port of Tampico on questionable charges, Wilson used the affair as a pretext for occupying the important port of Veracruz in April 1914. This action was an important catalyst in the downfall of Huerta since many European arms destined for Huerta's forces passed through Veracruz. Defeated militarily and with no political base, Huerta resigned in July 1914.

The divisions among the three remaining revolutionary leaders, Carranza, Villa, and Zapata, still prevented the restoration of political stability. Carranza was the moderate—himself of the entrepreneurial elite from the northern state of Coahuila. Villa and Zapata were the more genuine revolutionaries, but even they represented different elements. Zapata and his followers stressed a very specific revolutionary goal, the redistribution of land. Villa, on the other hand, led an eclectic movement of the disillusioned from the northern states. The Villa supporters were less united behind a single issue but were unified in their quest to topple Huerta.

Though the Revolution was not to end until 1920, the postrevolutionary political system began to take shape as Carranza emerged the dominant figure in the wake of Huerta's defeat. Initially, Carranza called for a convention of all the revolutionary forces to be held in Aguascalientes in October of 1914. His plan quickly broke down, however, as the Aguascalientes convention was controlled by the more radical elements. Carranza asked his supporters at the convention to walk out, while he withdrew his troops from Mexico City to Veracruz. Given his window of opportunity and united by their common disdain for Carranza and his "middle-class revolutionaries," Villa and Zapata briefly shared power in Mexico City in late-1914. But Zapata soon grew restless and returned to his home state of Morelos, while Villa made his way north. By early-1915 the Carranza forces, under the able military leadership of Obregón, had contained and isolated Zapata in Morelos and had won a decisive victory over Villa in the battle of Celaya. Carranza returned to the seat of power in Mexico City and was officially recognized as president of Mexico in October by President Wilson.

The beginnings of an institutionalized, postrevolutionary regime—some would argue even the earliest roots of the ruling party—can be traced to the 1917 constitutional convention at Querétaro. Hoping to avoid the debacle of the Aguascalientes convention, Carranza banned any followers of his former antagonists (Huerta, Villa, or Zapata) from the 1917 convention. Yet even the "Constitutionalist" delegates approved by Carranza were a diverse group dominated by the so-called Jacobins. In general, the delegates were a conglomeration of highly educated, middle-class professionals who had been locked out of political power under Díaz.[8] These participants at the 1917 convention set the precedent for future political leaders in Mexico by using radical rhetoric in an attempt to add some revolutionary legitimacy to their professional backgrounds.

At Querétaro, Carranza presented a draft constitution, which was a manifestation of classic nineteenth-century liberalism and only a slight modification of the 1857 Constitution. But the Jacobin delegates succeeded in strengthening even further the anticlerical principles and adding entirely new elements. The three most important revisions of the Carranza draft, which remain crucial provisions of the Mexican constitution, included: (1) Article 3, providing for the secularization of education; (2) Article 27, allowing the return of illegally seized land, state expropriation of private property, and state subsoil rights; and (3) Article 123, establishing extensive and path-breaking labor rights.

Though Carranza was singularly noted for his lack of commitment to the revolutionary premises of the 1917 Constitution, especially agrarian reform, his administration did open the political system to a variety of organizational groups. The Federal Electoral Law of 1918, while limiting the franchise to literate males only, established minimal requirements for creating a political party. The latter provision encouraged the growth of parties and other political groupings. The numerous military factions began forming loosely knit political organizations, sometimes calling themselves parties. Carranza's Constitutionalist party was by far the most influential, but other parties and interest groups were founded.

Labor was one of the first groups to attempt to organize politically under the new constitution. A month prior to the March 1917 elections (which Carranza had called in order to be elected president under the new constitution), labor leader Luis Morones and his followers formed the Worker Socialist Party (Partido Socialista Obrero, or PSO).[9] The PSO was a dismal failure in the elections and collapsed shortly thereafter. But in May of 1918 Morones, with Carranza's blessings, formed the first national labor confederation, the Mexican Regional Workers' Confederation (Confederación Regional Obrera Mexicana, or CROM). And in 1919 Morones helped establish the political wing of the CROM, the Mexican Labor Party (Partido Laborista Mexicana, or PLM). While the CROM and the PLM operated very much within the framework of the political establishment under Carranza, more radical labor elements founded the Mexican Communist Party (Partido Comunista Mexicano, or PCM) in 1919, which was one of the first communist parties established in Latin America after the Bolshevik Revolution.

The Mexican private sector was beginning to organize politically at the same time as labor.[10] In 1917 Carranza and A. J. Pani, his minister of industry, commerce, and labor, requested a meeting with Mexico City merchants to discuss issues of mutual concern. The Mexico City Chamber of Commerce then organized the First National Congress of Merchants in July 1917. At the formal opening, Pani declared that through this meeting "commerce had been incorporated to the Revolution."[11] By November the Congress of Merchants had evolved into the National Confederation of Chambers of Commerce (Confederación de Cámaras Nacionales de Comercio, or CONCANACO), which was to become one of the most powerful interest groups in the nation. The Mexican Industrial Center of Puebla, believing that manufacturing needed independent representation, asked Pani and Carranza to promote a separate industrial organization. As a consequence, the Congress of Industrialists first met in November of 1917, and within a year had established the Confederation of Industrial Chambers (Confederación de Cámaras Industriales, or CONCAMIN), the industrial counterpart to CONCANACO.

In 1920 Carranza attempted to handpick his successor as president. But Obregón allied himself with still another political leader from northern Mexico, Plutarco Elías Calles, in successful revolt against Carranza, who was forced to flee Mexico City in May. Carranza was assassinated shortly thereafter by a follower of Obregón. This violent change of power in 1920 marked the end of the Revolution and the end of an era in Mexican politics. Never again would violence be the instrument to gain power, and never again would a regime be forcefully overthrown by its opponents.

THE ERA OF CONSOLIDATION

Obregón was easily elected as the new president in 1920. At that time the three most influential parties, all supporters of Obregón, were the Liberal Constitutionalist Party (Partido Liberal Constitucionalista— the party centered in Mexico City that replaced Carranza's Constitutionalist party), the PLM, and the National Agrarian Party (Partido Nacional Agrarista, or PNA—a grouping of various agrarian forces and the most significant party in Obregón's political campaign).[12] Obregón enjoyed a wide base of support and did much to unify the country after ten years of bloodshed. His labor policy favored Morones and the CROM, and the largest labor group at that time responded by giving him unqualified support. In the field of agriculture, he distributed to the peasanty nine times the amount of land redistributed by Carranza. Obregón also stressed educational achievements, especially in rural areas, as more rural schools were built during his presidency than had been built over the last five decades.

Yet Obregón was more the consummate politician dedicated to consolidating national political power than the radical friend of labor and the peasantry. He suppressed the independent and anticapitalist labor unions and was the first Mexican president to use the state to control and co-opt organized labor. And his agrarian reform was actually a policy of caution and compromise. He never challenged the preeminence of the largest landowners, for fear that rapid and massive redistribution of the land would destroy Mexico's agricultural productivity. Finally, his political skills enabled him to bring many of the regional armies loyal to traditional *caudillos* under national control. This expanded military cooperation, along with U.S. assistance and the support of his labor and peasant allies, allowed Obregón to defeat a serious rebellion of Conservatives and disgruntled politicians in 1923. This revolt had been instigated by fears that Obregón's chosen successor, his secretary of *gobernación*, Plutarco Calles, would be committed to extensive agrarian reform.

The inauguration of Calles in 1924 was the first peaceful transfer of power in four decades. He came to power with the reputation of a somewhat radical liberal who would move Mexico even more in the revolutionary direction than Obregón. Calles did more than double the pace of land redistribution of Obregón, though the agrarian militants still were far from satisfied. In particular, while Obregón balanced urban and rural interests, Calles showed a clear tendency to favor urban labor over the peasantry. The PLM became the dominant political party, and Morones and the CROM prospered even more during the Calles presidency. Indeed, Morones was appointed secretary of labor and became one of the president's most influential advisors.

The greatest obstacle encountered by Calles was the opposition of the Catholic Church to his determination to implement the anticlerical articles of the Constitution. The position of both sides in this church-state conflict hardened, and the archbishop even declared a religious "strike" in which no church services were conducted for a period of three years beginning in 1926. The battle became violent as the so-called *Cristero* rebellion broke out, particularly in the western states of

Michoacán, Jalisco, and Colima. Though the rebels were defeated before the end of the Calles term in 1928, their movement was to have an important impact even after Calles' presidency had ended.

The presidential succession of 1928 provided a significant test for the Mexican political system. Though Calles' labor crony Luis Morones had aims on the office of the presidency, Calles seemed to have secured a solution by changing the Constitution to allow for reelection, so long as the presidential terms were not consecutive (the length of tenure was also extended to the present six years). This alteration was specifically designed to allow Obregón to return to office, and indeed Calles threw his support to the former president. Obregón was strongly favored by the agrarian interests, and though Morones and the PLM were quite reluctant in their support, Obregón was elected in July 1928. But only two weeks after the election, Obregón was assassinated by a right-wing religious fanatic (who had participated in the *Cristero* rebellion) during a victory banquet. The young assassin was sketching the portraits of the guests when he fired five shots into the head of Obregón.

Calles was the only leader with the prestige of Obregón, but his remaining in office would have stretched the revolutionary principle of no reelection too far. At this point in Mexican history, Calles made two decisions that had a tremendous impact on the postrevolutionary political system. First, he unequivocally announced in his annual state of the union address to Congress that he would permanently leave the office of president when his term expired later that year. This decision solidified the concept of no reelection, which still endures in Mexican presidential politics. He asked Congress to name a provisional president until special elections for a new president to finish the six-year term of Obregón could be held. An *obregonista* (who was also close to Calles) from Tamaulipas, Emilio Portes Gil, was chosen as the interim president. Second, Calles outlined the creation of a new national party (the National Revolutionary Party—Partido Nacional Revolucionario— or PNR) to encompass all the revolutionary factions and to institutionalize the succession of power. The PNR was the forerunner of the present ruling party, the PRI.

THE REVOLUTIONARY PARTY

In conjunction with creating a national mechanism to end the perpetual conflict among regional political and military leaders and to stabilize the transitions between presidential administrations, Calles wanted to create an electoral instrument that would allow him to continue to dominate the political scene. Three different presidents served during the six-year term (1928–1934) to which Obregón had been elected, but these were little more than puppets for Calles. Indeed, Calles came to be called the *Jefe Máximo* (the "Supreme Chief") during this period, which historians refer to as the *Maximato*.

The PNR was at first a relatively loose coalition of many regional parties and some functionally based interest groups. All the revolutionary organizations, except the Communists and Morones' PLM, sent delegates to Querétaro in March of 1929 to organize the PNR. The new party brought together the military *caudillos* (exemplified by General Abelardo Rodríguez of Sonora), the civilian *caciques* (such as Portes Gil of Tamaulipas), the *agraristas*, and some labor groups. Significantly, the PLM and the CROM were not included. After Morones had expressed his own presidential ambitions in 1928 and been so reluctant to support Obregón, his political career and the fate of his labor organizations began to deteriorate rapidly.

From the beginning the PNR was envisioned as a dominant, governing party. In the words of Portes Gil, who served as party president in 1930 after his time as provisional president of the nation: "The PNR is frankly a government party. . . . The Government has the program of the Revolution; the party has the program of the Revolution and of the Government. . . . The party will be a sincere collaborator of the administration. . . . This is the mission of the PNR and for this I say that the PNR is a government party."[13] Though the various organizations grouped under the umbrella of the PNR were given considerable autonomy initially, the party began slowly to reduce the independence of its affiliates and to centralize its own power. As one example, President Portes Gil ordered every federal employee to contribute seven days pay annually to the party. Thereby, the party was able to establish crucial links with the bureaucracy and an important source of revenue.

The first national party convention in 1932 at Aguascalientes altered the framework of the PNR in order to replace the loose organization of regional parties with "a hierarchy of municipal, state, and national conventions which were to decide policy and select candidates."[14] The organizational changes weakened the local political leaders while strengthening the hand of Calles and centralizing decision-making within the party. The Aguascalientes convention also reaffirmed the principle of no reelection. To demonstrate its political clout, in a short time the PNR managed to amend the Constitution to provide that no president could ever again reassume office (reversing the change that allowed Obregón to be elected in 1928) and that no federal senator or deputy could serve consecutive terms. This would insure frequent turnover in the decision-making positions and theoretically prevent the reconcentration of power in the hands of regional *caudillos*.

As previously mentioned, the three presidents that served between 1928 and 1934 were all subordinate to Calles, who continued to control

Mexican politics from behind the scenes. Calles first chose Portes Gil to be selected by a unanimous vote in Congress as the provisional president of Mexico. Portes Gil was a lawyer, a former governor of Tamaulipas, a powerful regional politician, and an *obregonista*. Thus, disputes among the military *caudillos* were minimized by selecting a civilian, and Portes Gil also helped bring many regional politicians into Calles' emerging coalition. Finally, the followers of Obregón were satisfied with the selection of a man from their own ranks.

In the fourteen months of Portes Gil's provisional presidency, the civilian politician proved to be somewhat more independent of Calles than his two successors.[15] He carried agrarian reform further than Calles preferred, and he strongly opposed Luis Morones. In fact, Portes Gil withdrew all government support from the CROM and the PLM and effectively destroyed the remaining political clout of Morones. However, by the time of the special election in 1929 Calles had created the PNR and was in a position to control events even more closely.

In this election Calles picked the relatively obscure Pascual Ortiz Rubio as the PNR's candidate to run against the better known and arguably more popular José Vasconcelos, the scholarly secretary of education under Obregón who was now running under the banner of the National Anti-Reelection Party. In the first of many questionable elections dominated by the revolutionary party, Ortiz Rubio outpolled Vasconcelos by the remarkable margin of over twenty to one in the official results.

The presidency of Ortiz Rubio was best characterized by his overt deference to Calles. Ortiz Rubio had no independent power base and was completely dependent upon Calles for his position. Tired of serving as the puppet of Calles, Ortiz Rubio tendered his resignation in 1932 after two years in office. To fulfill the remaining two years of the six-year term, Calles chose one of his closest collaborators and a military chief from Sonora, General Abelardo Rodríguez. Rodríguez continued the conservative bent of the *Maximato*, slowing agrarian reform, promoting the business sector and foreign capital, and maintaining the repression of labor. His only innovation was to bring a number of younger men into the government and the PNR.

Realizing the need to placate an increasingly restless left wing, in 1933 Calles endorsed Lázaro Cárdenas as the presidential candidate of the PNR for the 1934 election. Cárdenas had the requisite military background, rising to the rank of brigadier general by 1920. He had been a loyal supporter of first Obregón, then Calles, and had served notably in a long string of party and government posts: governor of Michoacán, president of the National Executive Committee of the PNR, secretary of war, and secretary of *gobernación*. Calles fully expected Cárdenas to be his fourth successive puppet president—and one who could placate the left. The latter objective certainly would be accomplished, but Cárdenas as president soon proved to be his "own man."

Cárdenas began to show his independence, and his determination to identify with the masses, even before his election by instituting a barnstorming campaign that was to take him to nearly every Mexican town in a period of a year and a half. Once in office, Cárdenas first consolidated his control over the military by increasing salaries and cultivating the loyalty of junior officers. Next he began purging Calles' supporters from high government posts. By 1935 the "Supreme Chief" began to feel his political power seriously threatened and publicly criticized the new president. His actions were too late to recoup his dominant status, however, and Cárdenas responded by sending Calles into permanent exile in the United States in 1936. This exile of the former strongman demonstrated the enormous powers of any incumbent Mexican president. Cárdenas was simply the first politician committed to establishing his political autonomy from Calles.

President Cárdenas quickly solidified his close relationship with the lower classes. He continued a practice he began as governor of Michoacán—that of personally listening to the problems of common factory workers and rural peasants. And he did more than listen. His was the first presidency to fulfill the aims of the Revolution, especially in the areas of agrarian reform and nationalization.

The six presidents prior to Cárdenas had redistributed some 26 million acres of land, but Cárdenas granted new land titles for over 29 million acres. Land reform under Cárdenas not only was quantitatively different from that of previous administrations but qualitatively distinct as well. He was the first president to attack directly the semifeudal *hacienda* landholding system, and by the end of his term he had effectively destroyed the economic and political power of the traditional *hacendados*. By 1940 about one-third of the Mexican population had received land under agrarian reform and most of the arable land in Mexico had been redistributed. Another important innovation of Cárdenas' land reform was to grant the land not to individuals as private property but to communities as so-called *ejidos*. The *ejido* land was communal property often farmed collectively but sometimes reapportioned to individuals. However, in all cases the land was only "bequeathed" to the people while the original title and ultimate control over the land remained with the state. Thus, Cárdenas achieved the demise of the landed oligarchy while creating a new class of peasant farmer that was beholden to the state not only for financial and technical support but even for the continued right to farm the land.

The other major accomplishment of Cárdenas was to implement the nationalization promises of Article 27 of the 1917 Constitution. First, Cárdenas enacted the 1936 Expropriation Law that allowed the state to nationalize private properties for "causes of public utility." In 1937 the state acquired the minority foreign interests in the National Railways of Mexico, and in 1938 Cárdenas nationalized the foreign-owned oil companies. The petroleum expropriation was probably the most celebrated act of the Cárdenas presidency, as it tied a commitment to labor rights with the nationalization of an important natural resource. After a lengthy labor dispute, the foreign oil companies refused to comply fully with the determinations of an arbitration board. Clearly siding with the workers, on March 18, 1938, Cárdenas signed the expropriation decree nationalizing the Mexican property of seventeen foreign oil companies. Although the U.S. government did not intervene militarily (as probably would have been the case decades earlier), negotiations for compensating the U.S. companies were difficult. In fact, the issue of compensation was not settled until the second year of the administration of Cárdenas' successor.

Expropriations of foreign and domestic property were not the only legacies of Cárdenas, however. Significant, though controversial, accomplishments were made in education. More federal expenditures were channeled toward the schools, especially in rural areas, than ever before. The Cárdenas presidency even affected what was taught in the schools. The PNR in 1933 had called for the teaching of socialist doctrine in all the primary and secondary schools. Cárdenas toned down this commitment in order to soothe the Church, but socialist education remained an important tenet of his administration.

The socialism of Cárdenas was perhaps best exemplified by his pro-labor policies, particularly his favoritism toward Vicente Lombardo Toledano, who was one of the most leftist associates of Morones in the early days of the labor movement. Lombardo Toledano left the CROM in 1928 to establish the General Confederation of Workers and Peasants of Mexico (Confederación General de Obreros y Campesinos de México, or CGOCM). The CGOCM grew to become the strongest labor organization and was the springboard from which Lombardo Toledano, with the encouragement and support of Cárdenas, formed the Confederation of Mexican Workers (Confederación de Trajabadores de México, or CTM) in 1935. Even at its inception the CTM was Mexico's central labor confederation which initially brought together approximately 3,000 unions and 600,000 workers. In a few years its membership had grown to over 1 million, representing some 15 percent of the Mexican labor force. Besides fostering the organization of more workers, Cárdenas favored labor with higher wages and better working conditions and consistently sided with employees in labor-management disputes.

The crowning political achievement of Cárdenas was the reorganization of the PNR into a more institutionalized, centralized, and expanded party. To represent peasant interests, and to serve as a counterweight to the CTM, Cárdenas had the PNR create peasant leagues in each state composed of the *ejidatarios* (peasant recipients of land). In 1938 these state organs were united into the National Peasant Confederation (Confederación Nacional Campesina, or CNC), the agrarian equivalent to the CTM. Peasants and industrial labor were to be two economic partners in Cárdenas' newly organized party. The third economic entity was the "popular sector," which was a much more heterogeneous group than the other two. This popular sector has often been described as representing the middle class, but more accurately it was designed to include most economic associations not already affiliated with the other two sectors. The core of the popular sector was the Federation of Unions of Workers in the Service of the State (Federación de Sindicatos de Trabajadores al Servicio del Estado, or FSTSE), which represented white-collar employees of state and national government (bureaucrats). But the popular sector also included some nonindustrial unions, cooperatives, associations of small businessmen and other professionals, youth groups, and individuals who did not belong to either the labor or peasant sectors.

In the mid-1930s, these functional groupings were beginning to assert themselves informally within the PNR. And in the congressional elections of 1937 many of the deputies elected by the party represented these economic sectors. Wanting to broaden the base of support for the party, in 1937 Cárdenas flirted first with the idea of forming a workers' party and then with the possibility of creating a "popular front" or antifascist party. Finally, he decided to transform the PNR into a corporatist structure organized around four functional sectors: the aforementioned labor, peasants, and popular sectors along with the military. Thus, on March 30, 1938 (shortly after the oil expropriation), the new Party of the Mexican Revolution (Partido de la Revolución Mexicana, or PRM) replaced the PNR.

The signatories of the pact creating the PRM as a corporatist body included (1) the *campesino* organizations that would form the CNC five months later; (2) several labor organizations including the CTM (the largest labor confederation), the CROM (reconstituted under new leadership), the Confederación General de Trabajadores (an old anarchist labor confederation), and the independent miners and electrical workers unions; (3) the disparate elements of the popular sector headed by the FSTSE (in 1943 these diverse groups finally created the National Confederation of Popular Organizations—Confederación Nacional de Organizaciones Populares, or CNOP—to coordinate their efforts); and (4) individual members of the army and the marines. The most controversial decision was the incorporation of a military sector. Critics argued that the military had never had an official role in national politics and that the creation of a military wing of the ruling party was a bad precedent. Cárdenas countered that the creation of a military sector in the party only recognized the obvious political involvement of the armed services and would eliminate any centrifugal tendencies of the military.

3

The Revolutionary Party in Power

The twin accomplishments of political stability and economic growth were not achieved until the postwar period. Two decades after the formulation of the 1917 Constitution, Cárdenas finally had delivered, at least in part, on the revolutionary promises of economic equity and political inclusion. But political order and economic "takeoff" still were not firmly entrenched. When Cárdenas left the presidency in 1940, the revolutionary period of Mexican political history unofficially came to an end. The Revolution was about to become "institutionalized," and the ruling party was about to be reorganized and even renamed to reflect this new direction.

At the end of his term, much speculation centered on whether Cárdenas would attempt to stay in power past 1940 or possibly anoint a fellow radical as the next president (such as Francisco Múgica, whom many expected Cárdenas to favor). However, Cárdenas surprised his critics as he picked his secretary of war, General Manuel Avila Camacho, as the PRM candidate in the 1940 elections. Avila Camacho was a moderate who had worked his way up through the military bureaucracy. His opponent was General Juan Andreu Almazán—the most senior officer in the army and a wealthy landowner very close to the Church hierarchy. Alienated by the policies of Cárdenas, Almazán had become a dissident within the "revolutionary family." To oppose the PRM in 1940, he ran under the banner of the Revolutionary Party of National Unification (Partido Revolucionario de Unificación Nacional) and also received the support of the newly organized National Action Party (Partido Acción Nacional, or PAN). Almazán, with his strong support from business, the military, the Church, and other conservatives, represented a serious threat to the dominant coalition, which overreacted by exaggerating the margin of Avila Camacho's victory.

Although the official results showed the lackluster Avila Camacho winning with an amazing 93.89 percent of the votes, the actual results were certainly much closer.

The election of Avila Camacho marked a distinctive shift from the populism of the 1930s. The institutionalization of the Revolution and of the official party had begun. Though Cárdenas had already toned down the strident anticlericalism of Calles, Avila Camacho moved even closer to the Church when he stated during his campaign, "I am a believer." This public profession of faith did much to bridge the gap that had evolved between the leadership of the ruling party and the traditional powers of the Church. In a further rebuff to the implementation of the revolutionary principles of the 1917 Constitution, land reform slowed considerably and private ownership was emphasized over the *ejidos*. Another major social intitiative of Cárdenas, the implementation of socialist education, was scrapped, although education was still a priority, especially in terms of attacking the problem of illiteracy.

Some of the greatest changes were in the realm of economic policies, as Avila Camacho set the stage for the Mexican "economic miracle." A major objective of the new administration was to placate the owners of expropriated property. Claims of U.S. and British oil companies were all settled by the mid-1940s. Also, the Mexican-American General Agreement of 1941 resolved the claims of U.S. owners of expropriated land. After the hostility directed at these foreign elements during the previous administration, Avila Camacho apparently saw a need to mollify foreign investors. Domestically, he also adopted policies favorable to private entrepreneurs. Though he continued to invest considerable sums in the public sector, the goal was to promote economic growth and to stimulate industrialization. The National Development Bank (Nacional Financiera, or NAFINSA) was strengthened and, in one of its most important actions, acquired the Altos Hornos de México iron and steel plant. Avila Camacho also initiated the first major programs designed to promote and protect private Mexican industries.

The ruling party was also reorganized (and even saw its second, and final, name change) under Avila Camacho. Only two years after its incorporation within the party, the military sector was disbanded. Avila Camacho (the last military person to serve as president) was aware of the controversy surrounding the military's role in the party, wanted to emphasize the apolitical status of the armed services, and believed that the political activities of individual soldiers would harm military cohesion. So the military sector disappeared, leaving the three functional sectors of labor, peasants, and the middle class. The balance among these sectors was also changing, with labor losing influence to the other two, especially the popular sector. As mentioned earlier, the CNOP was established to coordinate and strengthen the disparate groups that comprised the popular sector. At the same time as the influence of the middle class was being enhanced, the strident voice of organized industrial labor was weakened by the replacement of the Marxist Lombardo Toledano by the more conservative Fidel Velásquez. The lost political clout of labor was evident in the agreement of labor leaders to a Pact of Labor Unity through which labor promised no more strikes and accepted binding arbitration. Finally, in January of 1946 Avila Camacho officially recognized the moderation and institutionalization of the party of the Revolution by changing its name from the PRM to the PRI. At the same time that the PRI was born, Miguel Alemán (a civilian and former secretary of *gobernación*) was chosen as the party's standard-bearer for president in the 1946 elections.

Alemán produced policies even more conservative than those of Avila Camacho—thereby deepening the break from Cárdenas. He made industrial promotion an even higher priority with easier credit for the private sector and the introduction of import controls. He stressed more efficient operations in the state-owned industrial infrastructure (particularly the transportation system and the state oil monopoly, PEMEX), and he tried to produce a more "positive business climate." Of course, in the process he alienated urban labor (through the harsh repression of strikes) and peasants (by his lack of interest in agrarian reform).

Besides antagonizing the popular sectors by its economic policies, the Alemán administration produced three other significant political outcomes. First, the political clout of the military was further diminished. Alemán was not only the first civilian president since Ortiz Rubio, but he was also the first president to reduce the military budget to below 10 percent of total government outlays. As an example of the size of the military's proportion of the budget, under Carranza the armed services accounted for a full 70 percent of public expenditures; this had been cut to 30 pecent during the presidency of Portes Gil; and Alemán finally brought the military's share down to 7 percent.[1] Second, Alemán's conservative policies sparked the formation of a left-wing opposition party, just as the populist bent of Cárdenas in the 1930s had brought about the establishment of a right-wing alternative (the PAN). In 1948 Lombardo Toledano, the radical labor leader and outcast from both the PRI and the CTM, created the Popular Party (Partido Popular, or PP) as an opposition party on the left. The PP was begun as a Marxist-Leninist party to mobilize the masses against the policies of Alemán. Finally, corruption was recognized by almost everyone as becoming a major factor in the political scene under Alemán. Stories of millionaire politicians made rich by public graft and sacking their dollars away in foreign banks were plentiful in the immediate postwar period.

Despite the strong opposition of the lower classes and the widespread disgust with the growing corruption, in 1952 Alemán considered having the Constitution altered in order to allow him to run for reelection. Finally convinced that such a change was totally unacceptable even to party leaders, he next tried to promote the candidacy of Fernando Casas Alemán—the mayor of the Federal District who was ideologically close (but no relation) to the president. Unsuccessful in these efforts, he ultimately settled on his minister of *gobernación*, Adolfo Ruiz Cortines, as the PRI candidate.

The six years of Ruiz Cortines from 1952 until 1958 are usually described as uneventful. The most important consideration in his being chosen for the presidency was his reputation for honesty in previous public stints as governor of Veracruz and secretary of *gobernación*. In his inaugural address he pledged to cleanse the government of corruption and followed up by pushing for public financial disclosures and by firing a number of corrupt officials. His economic ideology and policies were similar to those of his predecessor, though not as extreme. Initially, Ruiz Cortines was somewhat less enthusiastic about private and foreign capital, since he was facing a slight downturn in economic activity in the aftermath of the Korean War. But a currency devaluation in 1953 boosted the economy and attracted new foreign investment. His presidency essentially attempted to consolidate the economic gains of the 1940s. The major political initiative of Ruiz Cortines, and about the only act of his term with true historical significance, was the extension of the franchise to women in 1953.

THE PENDULUM EFFECT

In the last years of his administration Ruiz Cortines began to realize that the issues of economic redistribution and social justice had been ignored for too long. The hierarchy of the PRI apparently agreed; and Adolfo López Mateos, the secretary of labor, was chosen as the party's 1958 presidential candidate in a clear shift to the left for the PRI. López Mateos was a young (47 when elected president) and dynamic leader who was close to the Cárdenas wing of the party. He defined himself as being "left within the Constitution."

The selection of the left-leaning López Mateos, after almost twenty years of fairly conservative and pro-business policies, provided the first evidence of cyclical policy shifts by PRI presidents, which have been labeled by some as manifestations of the "pendulum effect" in Mexican politics.[2] Briefly stated, the notion of a pendulum effect suggests that there are predictable shifts from one side of the ideological spectrum to the other as presidents succeed one another in Mexico. This argument posits that the political stability of the Mexican system is dependent upon the successful incorporation of all economic and political sectors. This process of incorporation in turn depends partly on periodic shifts between more "conservative" policies favoring the private sector and foreign investment and more "populist" policies tending to benefit urban labor and *campesinos* and to limit the penetration of foreign capital. Martin C. Needler first suggested that these shifts in policy (the swings of the pendulum) occurred over periods of two *sexenios*.[3] For example, beginning with a president on the left of the ideological spectrum, his successor (a moderate) would initiate the move to the right which would then culminate in a truly right-wing president following the moderate president. Then the pendulum would begin moving back toward the left with the next succession.

More recent extrapolations of this idea have emphasized that the ideological and policy shifts in direction occur with each change in administration. In analyzing the Mexican authoritarian state, Merilee S. Grindle posits that shifts in public policy coincide with each presidential change in Mexico: "In general, policy making in Mexico is an intrabureaucratic process which is clearly demarcated by the sexennial change of administration."[4] E. V. K. Fitzgerald also suggests that expenditure patterns in Mexico follow the pendulum effect.[5] And examinations of Mexican foreign policy provide additional evidence of the validity of the pendulum theory.[6]

One could argue that the period of institutionalization from 1940 to 1958 (the presidencies of Avila Camacho, Alemán, and Ruiz Cortines) represented the first pendulum swing, as policies turned away from the populism of Cárdenas in the 1930s. But the *sexenio* of López Mateos marked the beginning of the more rapid policy changes associated with each new president. In this scenario, the right-wing presidents included Ruiz Cortines (1952–1958), Díaz Ordaz (1964–1970), and López Portillo (1976–1982), while they were balanced by the intervening leftist presidencies of López Mateos (1958–1964) and Echeverría (1970–1976). Some empirical evidence suggests the Leftist presidents did heavily emphasize public investment, whereas their conservative colleagues leaned more toward favoring private investment.[7] Certainly, much qualitative evidence exists that since the 1950s the PRI has utilized this balancing act between the political left and right as one strategy in maintaining political dominance and stability. The qualitative contrasts between presidential administrations are fairly obvious beginning with López Mateos and extending at least until the last year of the López Portillo *sexenio* (1982).

As was the case with the previous leftist president, the populist ideology of López Mateos was most evident in his nationalistic foreign policy. The Petrochemical Law of 1959, the 1961 Mining Law, and the 1962 automotive industry decree were all quite nationalistic in their intent. Essentially, López Mateos was the first president to take the policy of "Mexicanization" (requiring majority Mexican ownership) seriously. He either nationalized or "Mexicanized" a number of crucial sectors: the telephone system, electrical power, mining, petrochemicals, raw materials and basic products, and automotive inputs. In non-economic foreign policy issues, López Mateos opposed the U.S. attempt to impose sanctions on Castro's Cuba, successfully resolved the so-called Chamizal controversy (the century-old border dispute involving the shifting of the Rio Grande farther to the south), and generally demonstrated the independence of Mexico from U.S. tutelage.

His domestic policies were not quite as spectacular, but he did place more emphasis on agrarian reform than any president since Cárdenas. Actually, on the domestic front López Mateos got off to a very bad start with labor and the left. Arguing that a railroad strike in 1959 threatened the security of the nation, he used the army to repress the strikers and he jailed a number of the union's leaders, including its powerful head Demetrio Vallejo.[8] Communist leaders were removed from other unions and the famous Mexican muralist and Communist, David Alfaro Siqueiros, was imprisoned on charges of sedition. Yet López Mateos ultimately proved to be the friendliest president to labor since Cárdenas. His most notable labor decision was to implement in 1962 a little-known article of the 1917 Constitution calling for profit sharing for labor. By 1964 many Mexican workers were directly benefiting from this initiative. Before his term was out he had even pardoned Siqueiros. And, finally, responding to increasing criticisms of one-party rule, in 1963 he amended the Constitution to insure greater representation of opposition parties in the Chamber of Deputies (the lower house in the Mexican legislature).

Speculation about the pendulum effect in Mexican politics was fueled further by the selection of Gustavo Díaz Ordaz as the PRI's presidential contender in 1964. Díaz Ordaz had been secretary of *gobernación* under López Mateos and was held responsible for the repressive policies toward labor and the left early in the López Mateos *sexenio*. He was widely regarded as one of the most conservative politicians ever to be selected the PRI candidate. Though his economic policies were not a sharp departure from those of his predecessor, on issues of democratization and political reform he did not disappoint those who viewed him as intolerant of political liberalization. Though he did implement the electoral reform of López Mateos, he actually took away congressional seats won in 1964 by the PAN. And in 1968 he annulled apparent PAN victories in mayoral races in Tijuana and Mexicali due to alleged electoral fraud. Díaz Ordaz' brand of "conservatism" was to halt any trends toward opening the political system, even if the major opposition was from the right wing.

Political democratization within the PRI was also stymied. Díaz Ordaz had appointed the reformist Carlos Madrazo as the new president of the PRI in 1964. Madrazo soon initiated a program of democratization within the party designed to enhance the participation of the rank and file and to diminish the influence of the traditional party bosses. The Madrazo reforms in the mid-1960s were roughly the Mexican equivalent to the McGovern-Fraser reforms of the early-1970s within the Democratic party in the United States. The major difference was that the Madrazo initiatives were scrapped by the party leadership before they could be implemented, whereas the McGovern-Fraser reforms were implemented and directly contributed to the nomination of George McGovern in 1972. Specifically, Madrazo had proposed opening up the nominating system for local and state offices to the party rank and file. The entrenched leadership of the PRI, particularly at the state level, protested vigorously and prevailed upon Díaz Ordaz to remove Madrazo within a year.

The most significant and tragic example of political repression under Díaz Ordaz was the case of student protests in 1968 culminating in the so-called Tlatelolco Massacre. Student discontent with the Díaz Ordaz government was strong as early as 1966 when a student strike at the National University (UNAM) produced the resignation of the rector. Events escalated in 1968 as Mexico neared the date of the Summer Olympics which it was hosting (the first Third World nation to host the games). The problems began with an insignificant fight in July between students of a college preparatory school and a nearby vocational school. The mayor of the Federal District, General Alfonso Corona del Rosal (who was considered a serious presidential possibility in 1970), overreacted by sending in the *granaderos*, a paramilitary riot police with a tarnished reputation.[9] The use of force was considered excessive and even unnecessary by many, and when students and *granaderos* clashed again in Mexico City on the July 26 anniversary of Castro's attack on the Moncada and Bayamo barracks, a major riot took place. Demonstrations against the government escalated during the coming months, and Díaz Ordaz and the protestors were moving further apart rather than seeking solutions or compromises. In late August the students organized the largest antigovernment demonstration ever with 500,000 people massed in the large square (the Zócalo) adjoining the National Palace. In mid-September Díaz Ordaz ordered 10,000 troops to seize the National University in order to dislodge students who threatened to disrupt the Olympics. The hostilities climaxed on October 2 at the Plaza de las Tres Culturas, also known as Tlatelolco, in Mexico City. This day has become the darkest memory in postwar Mexican history.

The Plaza de las Tres Culturas (Plaza of Three Cultures) is an important tourist, administrative, and residential area in Mexico City. Its name derives from the fact that the three cultures of Mexico (the indigenous, the Spanish, and the modern) are all represented within shouting distance of one another. Since this Plaza is a well-known focal point in Mexico City and also home to scores of lower-income people, the students called for another outdoor rally at the site on October 2. The demonstration was not terribly large and apparently peaceful until army and police personnel entered the Plaza in tanks and other armed vehicles and ordered the protestors to disperse. Tear gas was first used against the students, but soon the armed forces, utilizing helicopters and automatic weapons, fired into the crowds, killing hundreds of unarmed citizens.

The official explanation was that the police and army were provoked to open fire by snipers, but the results were the deaths of at least 400 citizens and the arrests of over 2,000 more. The hospitals and jails of Mexico City were overflowing in the aftermath of the army attack at Tlatelolco. The violence and severity of the repression were extraordinary in postwar Mexico, and the regime of Díaz Ordaz will always be marred by the tragedy of that night. Though he achieved some important economic and social successes, Díaz Ordaz is remembered by most Mexicans as their most unpopular postwar president, largely due to the killings of Tlatelolco.

Continuing the recent tradition of selecting the secretary of *gobernación* as the presidential candidate, Luis Echeverría was tapped as the PRI nominee in 1970. Echeverría was a close associate of Díaz Ordaz, had a conservative reputation, and was seen by many as responsible for the murders at Tlatelolco. Echeverría's background also portended what may be the greatest challenge facing the PRI today: the rise of *técnicos* with purely administrative experience and the fall of *políticos* who have risen through the ranks of the three sectors of the party and/or who have held elective posts. Though he did have strong ties to the PRI, Echeverría's governmental career was solely in administrative or bureaucratic posts, and he had never held elective office before assuming the presidential sash.

Despite his rightist credentials and past record, Echeverría surprised many by moving dramatically to the left and attempting to emulate a modern Cárdenas. This unpredicted shift provided more evidence for the pendulum theory. The principal tenets of Echeverría's new political agenda were income redistribution, an enlarged economic role for the state, controls on foreign investment, a hostile relationship with private business, and a foreign policy embracing Third World demands for a drastic overhaul of international economic institutions.

Echeverría was quite vocal in his support for income redistribution, though his policies often contained more rhetoric than results. Despite his lack of success, he seemed committed to revising Mexico's regressive tax structure. Wages did increase faster than consumer prices under Echeverría, and he made some substantial improvements in public housing. Also, Echeverría strongly supported emphasizing agricultural development, particularly the subsistence sector, in order to redress the growing imbalance between industry and agriculture. He increased credit to the agrarian sector, allowed higher prices, and expanded the role of Compañía Nacional de Subsistencias Populares (CONASUPO), the government marketing enterprise for basic commodities.

He produced more concrete results in enlargement of the public sector.[10] From 1971 to 1976 government expenditures rose much faster than the inflation rate. Total government revenue increased from 8 percent of GDP in 1970 to 12.5 percent in 1975, and the federal deficit of 1976 was over fifteen times as large as the 1971 deficit.[11] Much of the spending increases were in current expenditures, including outlays for housing, education, and agricultural development; but the most spectacular advances were in government-owned enterprises and public works. Echeverría committed substantial sums of public revenues to basic industries like steel and petrochemicals and even to the tourist industry by developing new coastal resort areas. This enormous growth in the public sector was not adequately financed and thus led to more borrowing abroad, growth in the money supply, budget deficits, and ultimately severe inflationary problems in the second half of the *sexenio*.

Some of the most far-reaching initiatives of the Echeverría government were several laws regulating foreign capital and technology. The most important aspect of the 1973 Law to Promote Mexican Investment and Regulate Foreign Investment was the requirement that *all* new firms have at least 51 percent Mexican ownership (expanding previous efforts at "Mexicanization"). Another 1973 law on the transfer of technology required the registration and review of all new contracts covering technology transfers from foreign companies. Finally, the 1976 Law on Patents and Trademarks limited the use of patents and required the use of Mexican trademarks rather than foreign names. These pieces of legislation served to control and restrict the entry of foreign capital and technology into Mexico and were the heart of Echeverría's unfavorable stance toward the growing role of foreign investment.

Echeverría's antagonistic attitude toward private capital was not limited to foreign entrepreneurs but extended to domestic business as well. As public expenditures and inflation accelerated, private investment and business confidence in the government diminished. The private sector became increasingly alienated from the Echeverría administration, and the various business associations and confederations even formed the Entrepreneurial Coordinating Council (Consejo Coordinador Empresarial, or CCE) to present a united front against the excesses of the government. Echeverría's treatment of the conservative Monterrey Group of industrialists was especially harsh. He continually berated them for not contributing to the overall development of Mexico, and the Monterrey industrialists were among his earliest antagonists.

In the short period from August to November 1976, Echeverría attempted to solidify his identification with the left wing within the PRI by coupling two sudden devaluations of the peso with the sharp and widely publicized attack on conservative business interests in Monterrey and with the expropriation of 100,000 hectares of fertile farmland in the northwestern states of Sonora and Sinaloa (the Yaqui valley). Such actions of the president created opposition throughout Mexico and also contributed to widespread confusion. One manifestation of the opposition was a one-day general strike of entrepreneurial chambers in the northwest in protest of the seizure of the land without compensation. The lack of support and the uncertainty of the political situation became so severe that rumors of a military coup were circulating. The inauguration of López Portillo less than two weeks after the expropriations was a welcome relief to many Mexicans.

Echeverría's shift to the left was also evident in his foreign policy, particularly in regard to international economic issues. Under Echeverría, Mexico assumed a leading position within the Third World quest for a New International Economic Order (NIEO) that would more justly deal with the problems facing the less developed nations and allow more Third World input to international economic decisions. His first step in formulating his *tercermundista* approach was an October 1971 speech before the United Nations in which he made a strong appeal for Third World solidarity. He followed this in April of 1972 with the delivery of his Charter of the Economic Rights and Duties of States to UNCTAD III in Santiago, Chile. The Charter was a strong statement of Third World demands for a global redistribution of wealth and more than anything else etablished Mexico's leadership role among the less developed countries in the ongoing North-South debate. Throughout his term he continued to push these ideas in various international forums. Even out of office, Echeverría attempted to take up the cause of the NIEO. Though he failed to gain the post of secretary-general of the United Nations as he had hoped, he did find useful platforms through his appointments as Mexico's ambassador-at-large to the Third World and later as its representative to UNESCO. He also created a Third World Institute in Mexico to analyze issues relevant to the NIEO.

The rationale for Echeverría's embrace of leftist policies seems to lie in his desire to pacify the increasingly restless left wing of the political spectrum and to make amends for the tragedy of October 2, 1968. He reached out specifically to his student critics in a number of ways. Many of those arrested in the aftermath of Tlatelolco were released, and more than a few leftist professors and intellectuals were actually brought into the government. The voting age was lowered to eighteen, and the minimum ages for serving in the Senate and the Chamber of Deputies were also lowered.

Yet these attempts at reconciliation with his youthful critics also exposed his growing difficulties with the political "establishment." In a major embarrassment of Echeverría, a hired gang of thugs (*Los Halcones*, or the Falcons) in June of 1971 attacked a group of student demonstrators with whom Echeverría purportedly was going to meet and extend his support. Such gangs are usually instruments of right-wing politicians (often entrenched party leaders) wanting to intimidate and harass independent leftist elements. A common belief is that *Los Halcones* were responsible to leaders of the CTM as well as to officials in the ministry of *gobernación* and in the government of the Federal District.[12]

In addition to these conservative pressures Echeverría also was plagued with political terrorism from the far left. Apparently his overtures to progressive forces were not sufficient to placate the more extremist groups. Many robberies and kidnappings of a political nature occurred during Echeverría's term, including the 1974 kidnapping of his father-in-law (a former governor of Jalisco) and the killing of the wealthy and influential Monterrey industrialist, Eugenio Garza Sada. A rural guerrilla force even operated in the mountainous state of Guerrero, and some 10,000 troops required over a year to capture the relatively small band and its leader.

José López Portillo came to power in 1976 determined to restore economic and political confidence in Mexico after the tumultuous years of the Echeverría administration. The latter's term ended in near chaos with the sudden devaluations of the peso, the shocking expropriations of rich farmland in the northwest, the near total alienation of the private sector, and genuine concern about the stability of the presidential succession. But López Portillo was inaugurated as planned on December 1, 1976, and quickly moved to restore political calm and to reassure the private sector. Once again, the pendulum swung back to the right.

As Echeverría can be interpreted as responding to political pressures to placate the leftist groups in the aftermath of the conservative policies of Díaz Ordaz and the Tlatelolco killings, López Portillo also appeared to realize the need to restore a political balance by appealing to the groups alienated by Echeverría. He wanted to renew the confidence of the private sector, halt the inflationary spiral, and restore the pattern of economic growth based upon a healthy industrial sector. The key to his strategy was restoring the confidence and the cooperation of business groups, and he wasted no time in establishing better relations with the private sector. His inauguration speech emphasized the calming of political forces and the need to rely more on private industry.

The ties between López Portillo and private business were developing into what he called the Alliance for Production, which was to stress joint planning between the private and public sectors. Some of the initial policy decisions associated with the Alliance for Production were stricter control of public expenses, tax exemptions for export products of firms owned wholly by Mexicans, reduction of taxes on enterprises, and increased prices for basic goods. As the Alliance for Production became more solidified, Mexican businesses continued to profess their support of López Portillo. In April 1977 the Monterrey Group, which had been so hostile to Echeverría, pledged its cooperation with the new government and announced a program to invest 100 billion pesos in Mexico over the following six years. In turn López Portillo stressed the contrasts between his *sexenio* and the previous one by describing the Monterrey industrialists as "profoundly nationalist." The national federation of chambers of commerce and industry capped his first year in office by issuing a ten-point program of concessions timed to coincide with the president's first state of the union address. Among the principal concessions to the government were promises to increase wages, hold down prices, and acccelerate investment.

The emphasis on financial conservatism was evident in the first three budgets of López Portillo. Though not willing to sacrifice economic growth, which rebounded in 1978 after two years of negative per capita growth, the spending policies from 1977 to 1979 were generally deflationary. After steadily increasing throughout Echeverría's *sexenio*, the federal deficit diminished in 1977. The absolute value of the deficit increased again in 1978 and 1979, but the deficit expressed as a percent of GDP steadily decreased from 1976 to 1979. The projected budgets for 1978 and 1979 were slightly less restrictive than the 1977 budget, which had no increase in real terms. The 1978 projections were for a 24 percent nominal increase and 10 percent real increase in federal spending, and the 1979 budget planned for a 23 percent nominal increase and 6 percent real increase. Significantly, most of the increases were not for current expenditures but for capital investment, especially in petroleum. The state oil company (PEMEX) was to receive 60 percent of total public investment in 1978 and the biggest single chunk (20 percent) of total public expenditures in 1979. During the boom years of 1980 and 1981, the federal budget was more expansionist, but the 1982 budget was again conservative—showing no real growth over 1981 outlays.

López Portillo reversed the Echeverría policies of promoting subsistence agriculture and land reform. Though he refused to overturn the 1976 expropriation decree of the former president and believed it politically impossible to return the land to its former owners, he did respond to private sector concerns by providing just compensation for the land and assuring the large agribusiness sector that any future agrarian reform would concentrate on unproductive land rather than fertile and profitable farms similar to those seized by Echeverría.

The Echeverría initiatives on regulating foreign capital were also drastically altered by López Portillo, who achieved a more harmonious relationship between foreign investors and the Mexican government by interpreting the strict foreign investment legislation more loosely. Another policy area in which the favoritism toward the private sector was obvious was wages and prices. López Portillo was reluctant to control prices, yet wages were held down. Through parts of 1977 and 1978, the state kept annual wage increases in public enterprises at 10 percent, and overall wages increased slower than price levels. Price controls were removed for automobiles in July 1977, and nearly 150 basic commodities were freed from price ceilings in February 1978. In one of the biggest shocks to the population, petroleum and diesel prices were allowed to more than double in December 1981. In other areas López Portillo was content to rely upon voluntary programs of price control supposedly initiated by private sector groups in well-publicized programs in 1977 and again in 1979. Ironically, the president continually praised labor for its sacrifices and criticized the private sector for not fulfilling its promises under the Alliance for Production of higher investment and slower price increases. This theme was part of each of his state of the union addresses from 1977 to 1979. Yet official policies persisted in favoring entrepreneurs and allowing real wages to decline.

López Portillo altered Echeverría's foreign policy principally by creating a more welcome environment for foreign investment and by eliminating the sharp rhetorical attacks on the United States and "imperialist powers." López Portillo did make a number of nationalistic decisions (such as not extending the gas pipeline to the United States and refusing to join the General Agreement on Tariffs and Trade), and his personal relations with Jimmy Carter were noticeably strained. But even with Carter, the attitude of López Portillo toward the United States was much friendlier and more receptive than that of Echeverría. And despite disagreements in a number of areas, López Portillo established a cordial, working relationship with Ronald Reagan.

Political reform was a major priority of López Portillo, though the initiatives of his administration did not threaten the dominant power of the PRI. Generally, analysts have recognized that under López Portillo "political liberty probably flourished more than it had for at least several administrations."[13] Most specifically, he altered the electoral procedures in 1977 to provide for 100 additional seats in the Chamber of Deputies which would be granted to the opposition parties on the basis of a rather complex proportional representation formula. Also, requirements for registering as a political party were eased. Whereas only four parties participated in the 1976 elections, seven ran candidates for the Chamber of Deputies in 1979, and nine were on the ballot in the 1982 elections. The major opposition party, the conservative PAN, benefited the most from these political changes. In 1976 its share of the vote for deputies was 8.45 percent, and the PAN held twenty seats in the lower chamber. By 1982 the PAN was able to attract 17.53 percent of the votes for proportional representation deputies and won 51 seats in the lower chamber.

The first five years of the six-year term of López Portillo, then, were characterized by close and friendly relations with the entrepreneurial sector and political reform that boosted the influence of the political right. However, in 1982 López Portillo lurched to the left in a series of policy initiatives favored by labor and progressive forces: a wage increase in March that canceled the effects of a February devaluation, the postponement of debt payments and the first exchange controls in August, and, finally and most importantly, the nationalization of the remaining private banks on September 1. Faced with an economic crisis due to an overreliance on petroleum exports and an overheated economy, López Portillo chose to leave office in a blaze of populist glory. The bank nationalization in particular was a major blow to the business sector and a tremendously popular decision among leftist nationalists. The comparisons with Cárdenas' expropriations of the oil companies in 1938 were predictable. Thus, López Portillo demonstrated that the pendulum swings between the political left and right can occur within presidential administrations as well as between them.

Despite having etched his place in history with the takeover of the banks, López Portillo had created another crisis of confidence. In the fall of 1982 the private sector especially was only hoping for more "pragmatic" solutions from the incoming administration of Miguel de la Madrid. De la Madrid did not disappoint the private sector, and the constrasts between the policies of the two presidents in 1982 were as great as those in 1976. In his inaugural address on December 1 the new president criticized the "financial populism" of the last year of López Portillo and promised "realism" in economic policy.[14] His two major themes were economic austerity and moral renovation. The austerity was evident in the 1983 budget, which projected the deficit to fall from 16.5 percent of the GNP to 8.5 percent in 1983. Substantial tax increases were coupled with drastic reductions in expenditures. The exchange controls were also reversed within weeks after de la Madrid took office. Moral renovation really referred to a campaign against govenmental corruption. De la Madrid did accomplish more towards controlling corruption in his first year than any of his predecessors. Charges were brought against almost 100 government officials, including Jorge Díaz Serrano, powerful former chief of PEMEX and once considered a potential successor to López Portillo, and Arturo Durazo, the police chief of the Federal District. Both men served under and were very close to López Portillo.

Though de la Madrid was viewed as starting Mexico on the road to economic recovery and his moral renovation campaign was generally applauded as the most serious effort yet, ominous clouds were building on the political horizon. By early 1984, party leaders within the PRI were admitting they faced a "political crisis." Widespread speculation centered on the issue of whether the Mexican electorate had lost its unquestionable identification with the PRI as the party of the Revolution. Even within the party, *técnicos* had risen to the top, displacing the traditional *políticos* from various party sectors. Echeverría, López Portillo, and de la Madrid were all *técnicos* more loyal to the administrative bureaucracy than to the party hierarchy. The crisis for the ruling party manifested itself in the elections of 1983, which provided the worst defeat for the PRI in its history. The opposition was especially strong in the northern border states, where the most violent protests in years against the dominance of the PRI occurred in early 1985.

SUMMARY: THE PRI—PAST AND PRESENT

The previous chapter began by referring to the PRI of Mexico as the best example in Latin Ameica of a dominant single party that is not subordinate to any political group, leader, or ideology. It can also be seen as one of the most successful political parties in Latin America (including both single-party and multiparty systems) in terms of achieving institutionalization and political stability.[15] The party's accomplishments are all the more remarkable given the fact that it had no direct, institutional ancestors prior to its creation in the late 1920s. Many of the great liberal minds of the nineteenth century certainly did influence the ideology of the founders of the party, since such principles as church-state separation, agrarian reform, labor rights, basic political freedoms, and no reelection date to prerevolutionary days. But the Liberal and Conservative parties of that era did not provide an organizational base from which the new party could rise. The first institutional trace of the revolutionary party was probably the April 1910 convention of *anti-reelectionistas* that nominated Francisco Madero for president (see Table 2 for the historical highlights).

The Constitution of 1917 first enumerated the major ideological tenets that would become the philosophical symbols of the dominant party: secularism, nationalism, and populism. President Carranza and his major economic minister, A. J. Pani, did incorporate labor and business into the governing coalition, but the party system prior to 1928 was still very decentralized and generally weak. In that year Plutarco Calles an-

Table 2 Overview of the Historical Phases in the Evolution of the Mexican Ruling Party

Major Phases	Characteristics and Accomplishments
I. *Nineteenth-Century Precursors, 1821–1910*	*No Strong or Institutionalized Parties*
1821–30: Liberal dominance and 1824 Constitution	Political instability
1833–1855: Santa Anna and the Conservatives	Continued political instability
1855–1876: *La Reforma*, Juárez, Liberal ascendancy, and 1857 Constitution	Secularism and federalism
1876–1910: The *Porfiriato*	Economic liberalism, foreign investment, and political stability through repression
II. *The Mexican Revolution, 1910–1920*	*Demise of the Traditional Oligarchy and Birth of the "Revolutionary Family"*
1910–1913: Díaz resigns and Madero presidency	Anti-reelectionist movement
1915–1920: Carranza and the 1917 Constitution	Calls for political and economic reform, Constitutionalist Party, and incorporation of economic sectors
III. *The Era of Consolidation, 1920–1940*	*Establishment of the Ruling Party*
1920–1924: Obregón	Broad political base
1924–1928: Calles	Key labor support
1928–1934: The *Maximato*	Reification of concept of no reelection and creation of the PNR to encompass all revolutionary factions
1934–1940: Cárdenas	Agrarian reform, nationalism, and reorganization of the PNR into the PRM with four functional sectors
IV. *The Institutionalization of the Revolution, 1940–1958*	*Economic "Takeoff"*
1940–1946: Avila Camacho	Shift in the conservative direction, PRM becomes PRI with three sectors (military depoliticized)
1946–1952: Alemán	"Deepening" of conservative policies
1952–1958: Ruiz Cortines	Consolidation of economic gains of the 1940s and women granted the right to vote

Major Phases	Characteristics and Accomplishments
V. *The Pendulum Effect, 1958 to the Present*	*Periodic Ideological Shifts to Preserve a Political Balance and Contribute to Political Stability*
1958–1964: López Mateos	"Mexicanization" and profit-sharing
1964–1970: Díaz Ordaz and Tlatelolco Massacre	Most conservative president ever and political repression
1970–1976: Echeverría	Populism, nationalism, and expanded economic role for the state
1976–1982: López Portillo	Alliance for Production, political reform, and 1982 bank nationalizations
1982 to present: de la Madrid	Economic austerity

nounced the creation of the PNR (eventually to be the PRI) as the party of the government and of the Revolution. Though undoubtedly selfish in his motivations (wanting to create a mechanism through which he could continue to dominate Mexican politics), the efforts of Calles in founding a party to encompass all the major revolutionary actors cannot be underestimated. No other political leaders in Latin America have been as successful in establishing a political party that would help create political stability without resorting to brutally repressive measures.

While Calles may have been the institutional father of the party, Lázaro Cárdenas was the ideological father of the party's populist and nationalist image. In asserting his independence from Calles, President Cárdenas in his six-year term from 1934 to 1940 did more to implement land reform, nationalizations, and pro-labor policies than any other president. He even renamed the party (now the PRM) and established four functional sectors within the party (labor, "popular," peasants, and the military).

The presidential transition in 1940 marked a qualitative change in the direction of the party, as it became a revolutionary party in name only. The next three presidents were much more conservative than Cárdenas and were committed to the economic "takeoff" of Mexico and to the institutionalization of the Revolution. The PRM became the PRI in the 1940s, and the military sector was depoliticized and excluded from the party. Mexico had entered the postwar period determined to modernize its institutions and to achieve political stability with economic growth.

By 1958 the political order, economic miracle, and institutionalized party were all firmly entrenched—so much so that the regime was fast losing its revolutionary legitimacy. One of the solutions was to begin the political balancing act, referred to as the pendulum effect, in order to placate at various moments the more dispossessed members of the revolutionary coalition. For the next quarter century, Mexican presidents would oscillate from the political left to the right (at least to the extent that these changes were perceived qualitatively) so as to satiate the political appetite of first one group, then another.

By the time of the 1985 elections for federal deputies and several state governorships, the PRI had enjoyed 57 years of almost unchallenged dominance. However, with its worst electoral defeats ever in the 1983 elections and the surprisingly violent protests against its "victories" in the 1984 municipal elections, the PRI faced its greatest crisis. The remaining chapters of this book will explore the factors behind this electoral success as well as the challenges that presently threaten the ruling party.

4

Electoral System, Opposition Parties, and PRI Dominance

A cursory examination of the changes in the electoral laws and practice since 1917 suggests that the Mexican system has been gradually but preceptibly marching in a democratic direction. Pre–World War II presidents such as Madero, Carranza, Obregón, and Cárdenas received from 95 to 99 percent of the total vote.[1] And prior to 1939 no permanently organized opposition party existed to challenge the PRI. However, by the 1950s three opposition parties had been created with viable long-term prospects, and in the 1952 elections the PRI's Ruiz Cortines won "only" 74 percent of the vote. Three more parties gained registration in 1979 with two others achieving that status in 1981, so that nine registered political parties contested the 1982 national elections. And in those elections de la Madrid received the lowest proportion of voter support (71 percent) of any PRI candidate in history. However, despite the proliferation of parties in recent years and the lower vote totals for the PRI, the PRI has never lost a presidential election (and always carried at least two-thirds of the vote) nor a gubernatorial election and has lost very few elections for federal deputies, senators, and scores of state and local offices.

Changes in the electoral laws, particularly those in 1963 and 1977, have provided the veneer of respectability for the democratization of the Mexican political system. In its infancy the postrevolutionary Mexican state accorded a negligible role to political parties and greatly limited the right to vote. The 1917 constitution stipulated that federal deputies, senators, and the president would be elected directly; however, it made no explicit reference to political parties. The original constitution only alluded to the rights of political association granted to all individuals. The first electoral law, enacted in July of 1918, was quite restrictive in terms of the right to vote. Specifically, women and illiterates (a substantial segment of the population) were not granted suffrage. Although the regulations regarding the establishment of political parties were very loose, parties were given few prerogatives and a minimal role in the political process. In fact, the law encouraged the candidacies of individuals completely independent of the parties. Charistmatic leaders remained the dominant forces at least until Calles created the PNR in the late 1920s.

The Federal Electoral Law of 1946 was the next major revision of the electoral code, which for the first time described in full the registration process for the parties (administered through the ministry of *gobernación*) and the representation of parties in electoral institutions. Political parties were characterized as "associations constituted . . . by Mexican citizens in full exercise of their civic rights . . . [and organized] for electoral ends and with a political orientation."[2] The requirements for the legal recognition of a party were rigorous: at least 30,000 nationwide members had to be certified by the secretary of *gobernación* with the membership dispersed in groups of 1,000 or more in each of at least two-thirds of the 32 federal entities existing at that time.

The principal motivation for the law was the desire to discourage independent challenges to the PRI, as had occurred in 1940 and 1946. The PRI wanted to bring all opponents more closely under the scrutiny of the dominant party. This control was to be accomplished largely through the Federal Commission of Electoral Vigilance, which was instructed to implement the electoral law. The 1946 Commission was composed of the minister of *gobernación*, two other cabinet ministers appointed by the president, one senator and one deputy chosen by their respective legislative chambers, and two representatives of national parties selected in "common" by all the parties. The PRI could easily control all these appointments and thus was well prepared to "oversee" the electoral process.

In 1951 Miguel Alemán created the Federal Election Commission (Comisión Federal Electoral, or CFE), which continues to serve as the federal agency administering all elections. The original membership of the CFE was altered from that of its predecessor (the Federal Commission of Electoral Vigilance) so as to diminish the control of the executive branch and to emphasize the role of the political parties. The only executive branch representative was the secretary of *gobernación*; the two legislative delegates remained; and the representation of the political parties was expanded to three members. A second major electoral initiative of the 1950s was to grant the right to vote to women, which Ruiz Cortines accomplished in 1953 by reforming Articles 34 and 115 of the Constitution.

President López Mateos introduced the concept of proportional representation to the Mexican electoral system for the first time in 1963 by creating the so-called party deputies. He explained his reasoning by admitting that the opposition parties had not achieved easy access to the legislature and that the political system was too inflexible to provide many opportunities for minority parties. He maintained that the smaller parties have the same right to state their opinions as does the majority party, but he concluded that only the majority had the right to make policy decisions. The new system established two means for electing deputies. First, the traditional manner of majority rule in single-member districts still applied to the 178 electoral districts that had been formed after the 1960 census. In addition, any party that won less than 20 percent of the vote nationwide was qualified to receive party deputies. These minority parties were allotted five deputies if they had at least 2.5 percent of the vote total and an additional seat for every 0.5 percentage points above the minimum of 2.5 percent, up to a maximum of twenty seats. The party deputies then would have the same rights and obligations as the regular "majority" deputies. As anticipated, in the 1964 congressional elections—the first ones held after the reform—the representation of the opposition parties increased almost sixfold.

Electoral changes in the late 1960s and early 1970s attempted to bring more young people into the political process. In 1969 the voting age for all citizens, regardless of sex or marital status, was lowered to 18; and in 1972 the eligible age for deputies was reduced to 21 from 25 and that for senators to 30 from 35. At the same time the minimum percentage for gaining party deputies in the proportional representation system was reduced from 2.5 percent to 1.5 percent, while the maximum number of such deputies allowed each party was increased from 20 to 25. A final move prior to the extensive changes of 1977 occurred in the Federal Electoral Law of 1973, which further expanded the role of the parties in the CFE. Now each registered party was accorded one representative with a full vote in the Commission. A further concession to the opposition parties in this legislation was the provision of franking privileges and guaranteed free access to the telegraph system, radio, and television. However, the greatest changes affecting the party system were still to come.

In 1977 President López Portillo revised seventeen articles of the Constitution pertaining to the electoral system, and these were codified in the Federal Law of Political Organizations and Electoral Processes (known as the LFOPPE), which went into effect on December 28, 1977. In Mexico these changes have been referred to simply as "La Reforma Política" (The Political Reform), and they surpassed even the 1963 revisions in terms of their impact on the political parties, the Congress, and the electorate.[3]

Mexican political parties had slowly been acquiring greater legal recognition. The 1946 law had given them status as political associations with represesentation on what was then called the Federal Commission on Electoral Vigilance. Their presence on the CFE was expanded in 1951 and again in 1973. The reforms of 1963 created the party deputies for the minority parties, and various political prerogatives were granted to all parties in 1973. But the 1977 law for the first time clearly defined political parties as "entities of public interest" whose purpose was to promote the participation of the people in the democratic system.[4] The registration requirements for parties were changed to allow more parties legal status. Ever since the 1946 legislation, the executive branch through the ministry of *gobernación* had determined party registration.[5] But after 1977 the electorate was given the power to determine registration. Any party that attained 1.5 percent or more of the vote in a national election was granted full registration. The 1977 law also established "conditional" registration to allow an unregistered party to participate in a national election in order to gain legal recognition. As earlier mentioned, in 1979 three new parties won registration under this procedure, and two more were granted conditional registration in 1981.

The election of federal deputies was also substantially altered by the 1977 LFOPPE. The Senate, composed of 64 members elected for a six-year term in single-member districts, was left unchanged. But the Chamber of Deputies was increased to 400 members still elected for three-year terms. Three hundred of these were the traditional "majority" deputies elected from single-member districts by majority rule. The remaining 100 seats (called *plurinominales*) were elected from five regional party lists by a complex proportional representation formula. The five regions selected 25 such deputies each. Any party that had won less than 60 majority seats and that had candidates in at least 100 of the single districts was eligible for the proportional representation seats. However, the method for deciding the distribution of these seats was so abstract and convoluted that more than one opposition party official remarked to the author that the PRI was almost able to pick and choose the number of deputies given each party.[6] In any case, at least one-quarter (100 members) of the Chamber of Deputies was guaranteed to come from the opposition parties.

OPPOSITION PARTIES

By 1985 nine political parties (including the PRI) were able to compete in the congressional elections of that year. At least symbolically the changes in the electoral laws and the proliferation of political parties gave the appearance of a gradual democratization of the political process. Two of the nine were independent opposition parties of the right: the PAN and the Mexican Democratic Party (Partido Demócrata Mexicano, or PDM). The major opposition party on the left was the Unified Socialist Party of Mexico (Partido Socialista Unificado de México, or PSUM). Other leftist parties included the Revolutionary Party of the Workers (Partido Revolucionario de los Trabajadores, or PRT), the Socialist Party of the Workers (Partido Socialista de los Trabajadores, or PST), the Popular Socialist Party (the Partido Popular Socialista, or PPS), and the Mexican Workers' Party (Partido Mexicano de los Trabajadores, or PMT). Finally, the Authentic Party of the Mexican Revolution (Partido Auténtico de la Revolución Mexicana, or PARM) was a relatively insignificant party that was closely aligned with the PRI. As shown in Table 3, the only real threat to the PRI in 1985 (and previous years as well) was the PAN. The PSUM received the third highest vote total, but its electoral support was less than anticipated. No other party received over 3 percent of the 1985 vote. In order to understand better the degree of liberalization in the system and the position of the ruling party, the backgrounds, philosophies, and successes of the opposition parties (particularly the two major ones) will be reviewed here.

Table 3 Political Parties Participating in the 1985 Elections

Party	Pronounced ideology[a]	Date of establish- ment	Date of regis- tration	% of votes for deputies 1985
PAN	Traditional liberalism; Catholic democratic	1939	1948	15.45
PARM	Revolutionary; nationalist; populist	1954	1957[b]	1.65
PDM	Democratic; populist	1972	1978	2.73
PMT	Democratic; anti-imperialist	1974	1985[c]	1.53
PPS	Marxist-Lenist; anti-imperialist	1948 (PP)	1960	1.97
PRI	Social democratic; populist	1929 (PNR)	1946	64.99
PRT	Trotskyite	1976	1981	1.25
PST	Social democratic; anti-imperialist	1975	1979	2.45
PSUM	Marxist-Leninist	1919 (PCM)	1981	3.24

[a]Ideology here is designed to reflect only the stated philosophy of the party, not its actual policy, preferences, goals, candidates, etc. Most of these descriptions come from González Casanova, El estado, pp. 78–79.
[b]Lost full registration in 1982 but received conditional registration for 1985.
[c]Conditional registration.

THE NATIONAL ACTION PARTY

The National Action Party was formally organized in September of 1939 by Catholic university students predominantly, but its founders also included many entrepreneurs and other professionals. Its roots can be traced to a number of earlier political and social movements, although its initial leaders were primarily motivated by reactions against the anticlericalism of the 1920s and the perceived radicalism of the Cárdenas regime in the 1930s. The earliest remnants of the PAN are actually claimed by some to be found in the movement of Francisco Madero.[7] The traditional liberalism of the PAN and its belief in a pluralistic democracy and in "effective" reforms are said to have been inspired and influenced by the *maderista* philosophy. Several founders of the PAN were even supporters of Madero or actual members of his government.[8] Another early political phenomenon that has been associated with the PAN is the presidential candidacy of José Vasconcelos in 1929. Many Catholics and other opponents of the emerging PNR dynasty rallied to the side of Vasconcelos. One of these dissidents was Manuel Gómez Morín, a former government official under both Obregón and Calles, a chief adviser to the Vasconcelos campaign, rector of the national university (UNAM) in 1933 and 1934, and finally the chief founder of the PAN in 1939.[9]

Even more important to the PAN than these political ties was its foundation in the more conservative and politicized lay associations of the Catholic Church. Three groups in particular had links with the PAN and its early followers: the *Cristeros* who rebelled against Calles in the 1920s, the semisecret corporatist organization created in 1924 called simply the Base, and the pseudo-fascist group that spun off from the Base in 1937 labeled the Unión Nacional Sinarquista (UNS). The *Cristeros* and the UNS were the most radical, with their support coming primarily from the peasantry. The Base was a somewhat more moderate and multiclass group committed to combating anticlericalism and communism.

Especially in its formative years the PAN was ideologically conservative and staunchly pro-clerical. The Party was born out of the 1930s struggle between the Christian right (led by Gómez Morín who organized the PAN) and the socialist left (epitomized in Lombardo Toledano with whom Cárdenas sympathized). The early *panistas* wanted to restore to the Church many of its prerevolutionary powers, especially in the areas of religious education and political participation. And they vehemently disagreed with the statist policies of President Cárdenas. Strong believers in the inalienable rights of private property, the PAN followers opposed the nationalizations and the agrarian reform achieved in the 1930s. The Party actually supported the redistribution of land which would grant peasants title to small, private holdings. However, its criticisms of land reform in Mexico focused on the collectivization of agriculture. The massive *ejidos* were seen to be philosophically indefensible and economically counterproductive and were cited as another example of the ineffective and communist-inspired reforms of the period. In the early 1940s the PAN shifted even further to the right, particularly in its foreign policy (with significant strains of pro-fascist ideology).

Yet the PAN of today cannot be classified solely as a political party committed to right-wing Catholic social thought and authoritarian political movements. It has chosen not to affiliate with the international Christian Democratic movement, and its present ties to the Church in Mexico are usually exaggerated. Furthermore, the PAN is quite serious about following democratic principles within its own decision-making processes and promoting those principles in the national political system. Contrary to the PRI, candidates and leaders for the PAN are selected in an open, pluralistic manner, and dissent and competition within the party are usually accepted. At the national level the PAN consistently argues for a more democratic Mexico and views itself as the best hope for creating a genuinely free system. It has criticized the history of political repression, presidential dominance, and fraudulent elections in Mexico, and on many occasions it has sided with the leftist opposition in a common struggle against PRI control.

However, the question of its own participation in the system poses the greatest dilemma for the PAN. Its presence adds legitimacy to the authoritarian one-party state, and so far the PAN has proven powerless in significantly altering the rules of the game. But if it chooses abstention as a means of protest, then it is vacating its role as the "loyal opposition" and allowing the PRI to monopolize the political debate. Since it has almost always chosen to participate, the PAN has played a very crucial legitimizing role for the PRI. When it did not run a candidate in the 1976 presidential election, the reason was primarily the inability to agree on a single candidate and not the desire to prevent the PRI from achieving its aura of legitimacy.

On economic and social issues the PAN in recent years has also not perfectly fit the model of a conservative party favoring free enterprise over economic justice and growth over equity. Certainly the Party's philosophy has been pro-business and oriented toward private ownership. But at least since the 1960s the PAN has also stressed social consciousness. In an important document issued at the close of the Party's twentieth national convention in 1969, the PAN advocated a third path of development between capitalism and socialism: *"solidarismo"* or, as described by one author, "political humanism."[10] Private property is viewed as positive so long as it also contributes to the society at large.

The indivdiual should not be alienated from his environment but has a responsibility to improve the general human condition. The Party's "Declaration of Principles" contains constant references to the common good, national harmony, the community, and the collective well-being of all Mexicans.[11] The Party even sees itself working in "solidarity" with the state to promote "order, progress, and peace."[12]

Since its inception in 1939, the PAN has nominated a presidential candidate in every election except 1940 and 1976. The PAN ran its own candidates for the first time in the 1943 elections for federal deputies. Its 21 candidates garnered 25,000 votes nationwide.[13] In 1946 it nominated its first presidential candidate, the former Carranza adviser Luis Cabrera. However, Cabrera refused the nomination, saying he was "too old and had too many enemies."[14] Its first genuine presidential contender, then, was Efraín González Luna, who won 7.82 percent of the vote in 1952. Since that time each PAN presidential candidate has received a successively higher percentage of the vote (see Table 4). In 1982 Pablo Emilio Madero, a nephew of Francisco Madero, was nominated and collected 15.68 percent of the vote—the highest total ever for the PAN.

The Party has also been steadily increasing its representation in the

Table 4   Presidential Vote by Party, 1929–1982

Year	PRI	PAN	PPS	PARM	PCM/ PSUM	PST	PRT	PSD	PDM	others
1929	93.55	—	—	—	—	—	—	—	—	6.45[a]
1934	98.19	—	—	—	—	—	—	—	—	1.81
1940	93.89	—	—	—	—	—	—	—	—	6.11[b]
1946	77.90	—	—	—	—	—	—	—	—	22.10[c]
1952	74.31	7.82	1.98	—	—	—	—	—	—	15.89[d]
1958	90.43	9.42	—	—	—	—	—	—	—	0.15
1964	87.82	11.05	0.68[e]	0.45[e]	—	—	—	—	—	0.00
1970	83.32	13.85	0.86[e]	0.54[e]	—	—	—	—	—	1.43
1976	86.89	—	3.65[e]	3.05[e]	—	—	—	—	—	6.42
1982	68.43	15.68	1.53[e]	1.03[e]	3.48	1.45	1.76	0.20	1.84	4.60

Sources: Comisión Federal Electoral, Reforma Política, vol. 9, pp. 128–29; González Casanova, Democracy, pp. 199–200; Levy and Székely, Mexico, p. 69; and Rodríguez Araujo, La reforma política, pp. 157–59, 144–48.

[a]5.32 percent for José Vasconcelos (National Anti-Reelectionist Party).
[b]5.72 percent for General Almazán (Revolutionary Party of National Unity).
[c]19.33 percent for Ezequiel Padilla (Democratic Party).
[d]15.87 for General Henríquez (Federation of Mexican People's Parties).
[e]From 1964 through 1982 the PPS and the PARM endorsed the PRI candidate, so their votes were actually votes for the PRI nominee.

Chamber of Deputies. Its first deputies were elected in 1946, and throughout the 1950s it retained at least five seats in the Chamber (see Table 5). With the advent of the "party deputies" in 1963, the number of PAN deputies increased to 20. And after the political reform of 1977 the PAN elected 43 and 51 deputies in the elections of 1979 and 1982, respectively. The PAN's delegation of federal deputies fell to 40 in 1985 8 "majority" and only 32 "party"), but the opposition parties claimed widespread fraud. Its delegation in the Chamber has always been the largest of all the opposition parties, and the PAN deputies have been the most significant counterweight to the PRI in the legislative branch.

In recent years the PAN has also been quite successful in a number of municipal electoral contests and actually poses the greatest threat to the PRI at the local level in those states where the PAN is the strongest. All together, of the 2,300 municipalities in Mexico, the PAN controls 33, and 22 are held by other opposition parties. But the most significant PAN victories have been concentrated in northern Mexico, where

Table 5 Representation in Chamber of Deputies by Party, 1943–1985

Year	PRI	PAN	PPS	PARM	PCM/ PSUM	PDM	PST	other
1943	147	—	—	—	—	—	—	—
1946	143	4	—	—	—	—	—	—
1949	142	4	1	—	—	—	—	—
1952	154	5	2	—	—	—	—	—
1955	154	6	1	—	—	—	—	—
1958	152	6	1	1	—	—	—	1
1961	172	5	1	—	—	—	—	—
1964[a]	175	2+18	1+9	0+5	—	—	—	—
1967[a]	176	1+19	0+10	1+5	—	—	—	—
1970[a]	178	0+20	0+10	0+5	—	—	—	—
1973[a]	189	4+21	3+10	0+7	—	—	—	—
1976[a]	196	0+20	0+12	0+10	—	—	—	—
1979[a]	296	4+39	0+11	0+12	0+18	0+10	0+10	—
1982[a]	299	1+50	0+10	0	0+17	0+12	0+11	—
1985[a]	290	8+32	0+11	2+9	0+12	0+12	0+12	0+12

Source: Comisión Federal Electoral, *Reforma Política,* vols. 9 and 10; Robert K. Furtak, *El Partido de la Revolución y la estabilidad política en México* (Mexico: Universidad Nacional Autónoma de México, 1978), p. 105; González Casanova, *El estado,* pp. 68–69; Levy and Székeley, *Mexico,* p. 70; Needler, *Mexican Politics,* p. 87; Rodríguez Araujo, *La reforma política,* pp. 148–49, 158–60; and Scott, *Mexican Government,* p. 243.

[a]The first number is the number of representatives elected in single-member districts. The second number is the number of representatives elected through a proportional representation system.

the PAN controls the mayor's office in Chihuahua, Durango, and Hermosillo (all are state capitals), Ciudad Juárez (the fourth largest city in Mexico), and eight other important cities.

After the 1983 elections that brought the opposition its greatest local electoral successes ever, the PRI reasserted its control in 1984 with sweeping victories in Baja California and Coahuila. However, the charges of fraud were louder than ever, and *panistas* in Piedras Negras, Monclova, and Escobedo (cities in the state of Coahuila in which the opposition claimed the PRI had committed widespread fraud) staged the most violent protests against the PRI in many years. The international bridge at Piedras Negras was closed down and municipal offices were set afire; and in Monclova the defeated PAN mayor refused to relinquish city hall until the state legislature finally appointed a neutral mayor acceptable to both sides. These incidents showed the growing strength of the PAN in the north and the determination of its followers to oppose what they perceived as fraudulent tactics by the PRI. The PAN was more confident than ever going into the 1985 elections for the Chamber of Deputies and seven governorships and even hoped for its first gubernatorial victories in the states of Sonora and Nuevo León. When the PRI swept all the gubernatorial races and the PAN received some 2 percent less of the total vote in 1985 than in 1982 (and 11 fewer federal deputies), the frustrations of the *panistas* in northern Mexico once against produced violent protests against the alleged electoral fraud.

Analyses of recent elections show the bulk of the PAN's strength coming from two areas: the northern border states and the more urbanized states.[15] Statistical analysis of the 1982 electoral results provides further confirmation for these conclusions. Table 6 shows the average percentage of the 1982 presidential vote won by the PAN, the PRI, and the PSUM, broken down into seven geographic regions. The strongest region by far for the PAN was the north, with the center and the center-north its second and third best areas. A variety of factors undoubtedly explain this relationship. Though the north provided most of the early revolutionary leaders, in the postwar period it has become more autonomous and isolated from the core area surrounding Mexico City. This separation has contributed to the feeling of alienation from the federal government held by many Mexicans in the north. In addition, the north has been traditionally more conservative, especially the industrial center of Monterrey, and more heavily influenced by the United States. For example, Monterrey is closer to San Antonio than it is to Mexico City. Northerners visit the United States more frequently and have easier access to U.S. radio, television, and other cultural factors. The sense of alienation, the economic conservatism, and the influence of the United States have all contributed to the increased vote for the PAN.

Table 6 Party Mean Vote, 1982 Presidential Election, by Region (in percentages)

Region[a]	PAN	PRI	PSUM
North	19.6	69.1	2.2
Center-north	13.8	75.1	1.2
Center	14.0	69.7	3.4
West	11.1	74.2	5.1
East	3.4	86.2	1.4
Southeast	9.3	84.9	0.6
South	4.3	85.1	2.6

Source: Comisión Federal Electoral, *Reforma Política,* vol. 9, pp. 96–127.

[a]The regions are broken down to include the following states: (1) North = Baja California, Baja California Sur, Coahuila, Chihuahua, Durango, Nuevo León, Sinaloa, Sonora, and Tamaulipas; (2) Center-north = Aguascalientes, Guanajuato, Querétaro, San Luis Potosí, and Zacatecas; (3) Center = Federal District, Hidalgo, México, Morelos, Puebla, and Tlaxcala; (4) West = Colima, Jalisco, Michoacán, and Nayarit; (5) East = Tabasco and Veracruz; (6) Southeast = Campeche, Quintana Roo, and Yucatán; and (7) South = Chiapas, Guerrero, and Oaxaca.

The identification of the PAN with the United States and with northern Mexico was exemplified in the controversy involving the U.S. ambassador to Mexico from 1981 until 1986, John Gavin, and PAN leaders. Suspicions that the U.S. Embassy during the Reagan administration favored the PAN were fueled in 1984 when several *panistas* attended the Republican Party National Convention in Dallas and when Ambassador Gavin met with PAN leaders and Catholic Church officials in Hermosillo in August. Many commentators in Mexico charged Gavin with interfering in the internal affairs of Mexico, and PRI President Adolfo Lugo Verduzco issued a stinging attack on Gavin. In the minds of many leftists, the PAN, the Catholic Church, and the U.S. Embassy form a united front threatening the progress of the ongoing revolution. Though the ties are considerably exaggerated by most Mexican leftists, the Reagan administration was undoubtedly sympathetic to the more conservative domestic and foreign policy stands of the PAN. And it was no surprise that Gavin met with the PAN in Hermosillo, one of the northern centers of power for the Party.

Independent of its northern base, the PAN attracts considerable support from urban areas all across Mexico. Again, the 1982 data confirm the conclusions of earlier studies associating a stronger PAN vote with measures of urbanization. In this analysis at the state level, the PAN's percent of the 1982 vote has been correlated with three measures of urbanization: the percent of the population in metropolitan areas of more than 80,000 people; the percent of the population in municipalities with more than 5,000 people; and the percent of the economically active population engaged in the manufacturing sector.[16] For each measure of urbanization the correlation coefficient with votes for the PAN is positive and statistically significant (see Table 7), and the strongest relationship is with the most urbanized areas (>80,000). If we divide the states into those above the mean value in terms of urbanization ("urban") and those below the mean value ("nonurban"), the association of the PAN with urban regions is even more obvious (see Table 8). The PAN receives from 18 to 21 percent of the vote (depending upon the variable) in urban states and only 8 to 9 percent of the vote in nonurban states.

The reasons for the relative strength of the PAN in urban areas are varied. For one, urban voters tend to be better educated, more sophisticated, and less vulnerable to socialization by the ruling party. The PRI has been most successful in controlling rural politics, while the PAN

Table 7 Pearson Correlation Coefficients, 1982 Party Vote with Urbanization (levels of significance in parentheses)

Variable	PAN	PRI	PSUM
Percent urban (>80,000)	0.7609	−0.8230	0.2300
	(0.000)	(0.000)	(0.103)
Percent urban (>5,000)	0.7157	−0.7287	0.1617
	(0.000)	(0.000)	(0.188)
Percent labor force	0.4977	−0.4947	0.0890
in manufacturing	(0.002)	(0.002)	(0.314)

Table 8 Party Mean Vote, 1982 Presidential Election, by Urbanization (in percentages)

party	Percent urban (>80,000)		Percent urban (>5,000)		Percent labor force in manufacturing	
	nonurban	urban	nonurban	urban	nonurban	urban
PAN	8.9	21.3	8.0	18.3	9.8	18.9
PRI	80.8	63.6	81.5	68.2	79.8	66.6
PSUM	2.2	2.9	2.5	2.3	2.3	2.6

has made its best inroads with the urban electorate. Urban areas also tend to be more developed economically with higher average income levels—demographic characteristics that suggest a natural attraction to the PAN's pro-business and pluralistic ideology. Finally, the urban centers are evolving rapidly and contain segments of the population (particularly in the middle class) that are emerging politically and economically, have fewer ties to the traditional political organizations, and enjoy more independence from the PRI. It should be noted that the PAN has had little success in attracting low-income, labor votes and has encountered surprising obstacles in its appeals to the upper class (whose voters appear to recognize that the PRI still controls the reins of power). Thus, the predominant PAN support comes from the urban, middle-class voter, who perceives the manipulative nature of the PRI and sees no rewards in being co-opted by the dominant party. These voters typically feel they have not gained their fair share of the benefits from the system and cast their lot with the PAN as a protest vote against the PRI.

UNIFIED SOCIALIST PARTY OF MEXICO

The second major opposition party in the 1982 elections was the Marxist-Leninist Unified Socialist Party of Mexico. Though officially created only in November of 1981, the PSUM is essentially a successor to the PCM and thus has a longer history than either the PRI or the PAN. Despite this long tradition, the Communist Party did not have much of a political impact, electoral or otherwise, until the political reforms of the 1970s and the establishment of the PSUM. Potential accomplishments of the PCM were also stymied by either internal strife or government repression.

The Communist Party was most successful in its earliest decades. After its founding in 1919, the PCM participated in many labor and peasant organizations: it organized the Liga de Comunidades Agrarias in 1924 and participated in forming the CTM in 1936. The popular front strategy in the 1930s brought new members, as the PCM actually reached its peak in this decade with its highest membership total ever (some 30,000).[17] Yet even in this period, the PCM was troubled with internal divisions, as exemplified in the expulsion of Trotskyites such as the famous muralist Diego Rivera.

With the conservative trend in Mexican politics beginning in the 1940s, the PCM began a steady decline in membership and also was purged from most labor organizations. Harassment and arrests by the government increased, and several splinter parties were formed. In 1948 the labor leader Lombardo Toledano formed the PP under the belief that a so-called nationalist party such as the PP would achieve more influence than an avowed Marxist-Leninist party. The PP came to overshadow the PCM in the postwar period, though the PP (and later the PPS, which became its new name in the 1960s) was not nearly as independent from the government as the PCM. A third party, the Mexican Worker-Peasant Party (Partido Obrero-Campesino Mexicano, or POCM), was organized in 1950 by a group of expelled PCM members. The goal of the POCM was always the reunification of the left, which it saw partially fulfilled in the 1980s when it joined the PSUM under its new name, the Movement for Socialist Action and Unity (Movimiento de Acción y Unidad Socialista, or MAUS). All three Marxist-Leninist parties supported the unsuccessful presidential candidacy of Lombardo Toledano in 1952, but in later elections the PPS, as a fully registered party, always endorsed the PRI candidate, while the PCM and the POCM retained their independence but remained outside the realm of legal political parties.

The PCM finally gained conditional registration in 1978 (and thus was legalized for the first time since the 1946 Electoral Law) under the new electoral reforms initiated by López Portillo. Allied with three smaller parties, the PCM gained legal registration after the 1979 elections in which it won 5.4 percent of the vote and eighteen proportional representation seats in the Chamber of Deputies. At a national party congress in November of 1981, the PCM officially dissolved itself; and a few days later the PSUM was created by the union of the old PCM along with three smaller parties that participated with it in 1979: the Mexican People's Party (PPM), the Revolutionary Socialist Party (PSR), and the MAUS. However, the PCM was unsuccessful in attracting the affiliation of the other leftist parties: the PPS, the PST, and the PMT (the Mexican Workers Party, an unregistered party). Thus, the left remained somewhat divided despite the unity attempts of the PSUM.

Since its inception, the PSUM has taken relatively moderate stands on major issues and has achieved considerable respect as a serious, democratic party. Though a revolutionary party, it advocates a popular, democratic, and socialist revolution. It has remained independent of Moscow and has been critical of a number of Soviet foreign policy moves (including the 1968 invasion of Czechoslovakia and more recently the invasion of Afghanistan and the repression of Solidarity in Poland). The PSUM would be appropriately described as a "Eurocommunist" party that believes in democracy and civil liberties and that remains independent of the Soviet Union. The PSUM has in fact encouraged its identification with the Communist parties of Spain and Italy.

The PSUM participated in its first national elections in 1982, running Arnoldo Martínez Verdugo (former secretary-general of the PCM) as its presidential nominee. Martínez Verdugo received 3.48 percent of the national vote, which was third behind the PRI and the PAN. But the PSUM was openly disappointed in its showing. In the Chamber of Deputies it was awarded seventeen of the proportional representation seats—one less than its total in 1979. In 1985 its proportional representation seats fell to twelve. Thus, the PSUM maintained its position as the second major opposition party, but it did not establish itself as a serious national threat to the PRI.

One of the greatest problems for the PSUM has been in building a political base. The usual cornerstones for a communist party, either the peasantry or organized labor, are already dominated by the PRI. The most significant support for the PSUM comes from students and intellectuals, who do not form a very formidable voting bloc. The analysis of PSUM support in the 1982 election confirms its lack of a clear political base (see Tables 6-8). Whereas the PAN has been especially strong across northern Mexico, the PSUM has no such regional support. Its best showing was in the west, with its highest percent of the vote coming in the state of Nayarit (11.0 percent). But this is a small state, not heavily urbanized, and hardly the springboard for a successful national campaign. The PSUM's next best states were the Federal District (7.5 percent), Jalisco (6.2 percent), Sinaloa (5.2 percent), and the state of México (5.0 percent). These are larger, more urbanized states, but still regionally diversified. The PSUM simply lacks a firm regional toehold to use as a starting point for building a strong national party. The correlations with the urbanization variables also suggest that the Party has not developed an identity with either urban or rural voters. The PSUM did somewhat better in the urban areas, but the difference was slight and not statistically significant. Without an established national following, the absence of an identifiable base of support (whether regional, demographic, or other) is indeed a negative factor.

The PSUM has achieved control in a few smaller cities and at least one case has gained international notoriety. In Juchitán, a town of 70,000 in southern Oaxaca populated predominantly by Zapotec Indians, a PSUM-affiliated leftist group (labeled the COCEI for Coalition of Peasants, Workers, and Students of the Isthmus) won the 1981 elections for city council and mayor. However, with state elections on the horizon, in 1983 the PRI began to crack down on Juchitán. The state government blocked funds for public works, and the federal government set up a radio transmitter to jam Juchitán's new station that had begun broadcasting in the Zapotec language. Violent clashes escalated between PRI and PSUM partisans, and after two demonstrators were killed in August, the PRI governor of Oaxaca blamed the PSUM mayor of Juchitán and named a member of the PRI to replace him. The socialists refused to relinquish city hall, and a special election was called for November to resolve the stalemate. One hundred state police were brought in to keep the peace but were unsuccessful in removing the leftists from city hall. The PRI was declared the narrow winner of the special election, but the COCEI occupants of city hall had to be removed forcefully from the municipal offices, with at least three people being shot. Once again the PSUM found itself with a noble cause but still without significant political power.

OTHER OPPOSITION PARTIES

The majority of the remaining opposition parties would generally be placed on the left of the political spectrum, although not all are genuine opponents of the PRI. The oldest of these parties is the PPS, created as the PP in 1948 by Vicente Lombardo Toledano. Ostensibly a socialist party, the PPS has evolved into little more than an appendage of the PRI. During his lifetime, the PPS was almost exclusively dependent upon the fame, charisma, and intellect of its founder. Lombardo Toledano had probably the most extensive involvement in organized labor of any political leader and was quite influential among the intellectual left. He had been an ally of Luis Morones in establishing the CROM, created the CGOCM and later the CTM, and served as president of the Latin American Labor Confederation and vice president of the World Labor Federation.

In June of 1948 the Partido Popular conducted its first national assembly and was officially born. Its first platform outlined the major themes that have remained central to its ideology ever since: nationalism and anti-imperialism (directed at the United States), regulation and control of foreign investment, more extensive state nationalizations, income redistribution, and agrarian reform. The Party ran its first candidates in 1949 for federal deputies and the governor's post in Sonora. The PP initially claimed victory in Sonora, but facing a government decision to the contrary soon abandoned its protest. This easy concession to the PRI caused the first defectors and the first accusations that the PP was a tool of the ruling party.

In 1952 the PP ran its own presidential candidate for the first and only time. Once again, however, it was criticized for being used by the PRI in that its nominee, Lombardo Toledano, was going to split the opposition vote on the left with the popular candidate General Miguel Henríquez Guzmán. Despite the support of the PP, the PCM, and the POCM, Lombardo Toledano received only 1.98 percent of the vote, while Henríquez won 15.87 percent. After the election, Lombardo Toledano threw his support to Ruiz Cortines, and the PP/PPS has supported every PRI presidential candidate and many of the ruling party's gubernatorial candidates since then. The Party officially added the label "Socialist" to its name in 1960, becoming the PPS, but in reality it was becoming increasingly dependent upon the PRI. It always justified the alliance by arguing that the PRI's independent and leftist foreign policy was ideologically akin to its anti-imperialist positions. However, the more acceptable explanation is that the PPS reaped considerable rewards for its support of the PRI.

The first obvious case of special treatment by the PRI-dominated government occurred in the 1964 elections. Though the PPS received only 1.37 percent of the vote for deputies (under the 1963 legislation a minimum of 2.5 percent was required for representation), the PRI-dominated Federal Election Commission literally gave the PPS one local deputy and nine "party" deputies in the federal Chamber. Its vote increased to 2.06 percent in 1967, and the PPS sent ten "party" deputies to the legislature. In the 1970 congressional elections its support fell to only 1.35 percent, but it still retained the ten seats. Even though its vote totals were minuscule throughout this period and by law were not sufficient to merit representation in the Chamber of Deputies, it remained the second largest opposition party in the Chamber until 1979. A deep split in the Party in the mid-1970s and the political reform of 1977 began its steady decline.

The deterioration of the PPS was inevitable when Lombardo Toledano died in 1968. He was succeeded as secretary-general of the PPS by Jorge Cruickshank García, who was significantly less influential and less respected. The PPS actually made its best showing ever in the 1973 elections with 3.46 percent of the vote and thirteen deputies (three local and ten "party"). However, events in 1975 severely weakened the Party internally and caused it to lose whatever credibility it previously had possessed.

In the elections of 1975 the PPS claimed the first-ever gubernatorial victory over the PRI in the state of Nayarit. Its candidate, Alejandro Gascón Mercado, who was from a powerful family in Nayarit and was related to a previous governor, felt that he had defeated the PRI nominee. When the victory was awarded to the PRI, Gascón Mercado demanded that the results be nullified and a new election be held. Cruickshank, however, convinced the Central Committee of the Party to recognize the PRI victory. For his efforts, he was declared the winner of a Senate seat from Oaxaca and became the first and only non-PRI senator in Mexico's history. The blatant political favoritism thoroughly discredited Cruickshank, and in 1977 Gascón Mercado led a majority of the PPS membership out of the Party and into the newly formed PPM, which eventually joined the PCM in creating the PSUM. The Cruickshank led PPS then won a meager 2.8 percent of the 1979 vote and less than 2 percent in both 1982 and 1985.

Another party on the left, which has been more independent of the PRI, is the PST, founded in 1974 by former leaders of the 1968 student movement. Some even speculate that it was designed to fill the void left by the decline of the PPS.[18] The roots of the PST began with the formation of the Comité Nacional de Auscultación y Coordinación (CNAC) in 1971 by a distinguished group of Mexicans who had been involved in the railroad strike of 1959 and the student protests of 1968. The leadership of the CNAC included the union head Demetrio Vallejo, writers Octavio Paz and Carlos Fuentes, and engineer-turned-activist Heberto Castillo. Their policy positions included the traditional demands of the Mexican left: release of political prisoners, nationalization of the banks, exchange controls, firmer regulation of foreign investment, and revision of the electoral laws. In 1973 a group headed by Rafael Aguilar Talamantes split from the CNAC to form the PST as a socialist party committed to creating a broad national front. It is ideologically close to the left wing of the PRI and is often compared to the political leanings of former presidents Cárdenas and Echeverría. The PST achieved legal registration in the elections of 1979 when it won 2.2 percent of the vote and ten "party" deputies. In 1982, however, its vote total diminished to a disappointing 1.79 percent with eleven deputies. While it rebounded with 2.45 percent of the vote in 1985, it remains a weak party in the electoral arena.

Another party that evolved from the CNAC was the Mexican Workers' Party (Partido Mexicano de los Trabajadores, or PMT), led by Heberto Castillo and Demetrio Vallejo. A former engineering professor at UNAM, Castillo was jailed after the Tlatelolco Massacre and upon his release became one of the most respected opponents of the Echeverría and López Portillo administrations. Castillo was especially critical of Mexico's oil policies for not being sufficiently nationalistic. Vallejo, of course, led the railroad strike of the late-1950s. The PMT chose not to participate in the elections of 1979 or 1982, because it believed they were not fair or democratic. The PMT was negotiating with the PCM prior to the 1982 election in order to achieve a single presidential candidate for a unified leftist coalition. The most likely nominee was considered to be Castillo. However, the PMT backed out at the last minute and remained without legal registration for the 1982 elections. It did achieve conditional registration in 1985 and won six deputies with just over 1.5 percent of the vote.

The final opposition party on the left in the 1985 election was the PRT. It was formed in 1976 as the first Trotskyite party in Mexico and received conditional registration in 1981 and full registration with the election of 1982. Though it gained no deputies in that year, its presidential candidate, Rosario Ibarra de Piedra, garnered 1.76 percent of the vote, and thus the Party gained legal status on the basis of its presidential vote. As the first woman candidate in Mexican history, mother of a political prisoner, and well-known leader of a human rights group, her campaign attracted considerable attention. The PRT did win six proportional representation seats in 1985, even though its vote shrank to 1.25 percent.

Other than the PAN, two additional political parties have existed on the right: the PARM and the PDM. The PARM has been even more of an arm of the PRI than the PPS, while the PDM has retained its independence from PRI control. The PARM was founded in the early 1950s by a group of retired army generals somewhat alienated from the PRI. Whereas the PPS was intended to be associated with the left wing of the PRI, the PARM was clearly an appendage of the PRI's right wing. Its first electoral experience came in 1958. The PARM ran its own federal deputies, but it supported the PRI candidacy of López Mateos. In fact, since achieving registration in 1957 it has unequivocally supported every PRI presidential nominee.

As with the PPS, the PARM was awarded more "party" deputies than its voting support warranted. Its highest vote total in the three national elections between 1958 and 1964 was 0.71 percent, which was legally not sufficient even to be a registered party (counting each PARM vote as a PARM member). Yet the Party was registered, and in 1964 it was awarded five "party" deputies in the federal chamber (despite the fact that its vote total was less than one-third of the necessary minimum required for registration). In 1976 the PARM suffered some internal conflicts, and by 1982 its proportions of the national vote were reduced to 1.36 percent of the votes for deputies and 1.03 percent of the presidential vote. In the reformist environment of the post-1977 period, the legal registration requirement of 1.5 percent was finally upheld and the PARM lost its legal status. After the 1982 disaster, it abandoned its offices in Mexico City and did not appear likely to regain its registration. However, the PARM was resurrected for the 1985 congressional elections (undoubtedly with the PRI support) and even managed to elect two federal deputies from single-member districts.

The PDM is a much smaller party than the PAN, though they share some commonalities. Of course both are conservative parties with ties to the Catholic Church.[19] The differences between the two essentially involve class base (the PDM is more associated with *campesinos* and the PAN with small business) and religious affiliation (the PDM is more blatantly pro-clerical). The PDM really traces its roots back to 1937 and the formation of the UNS in León, Guanajuato. Since the UNS is a religious organization, it cannot participate in politics under the Mexican Constitution. Thus, it has attempted on various occasions to create a party to represent its philosophy in the political arena. Three times in the past—1946, 1953, and 1963—it has failed to sustain a registered party. Either legal registration was denied or the party was stripped of its legal status soon after its establishment. The PDM, created in 1972, was the fourth and most successful attempt by the UNS to create a political arm.

The PDM gained conditional registration in 1978 and full registration in 1979. Campaigning under its ideology emphasizing the Catholic Church, the family, the individual, and private party, the PDM acquired ten "party" deputies in 1979 and twelve in both 1982 and 1985. Its share of the vote has consistently fluctuated around 2 percent. It is particularly strong in the west (the so-called *Bajío* region where the *Cristero* rebellion was centered and the UNS is concentrated) and the center-north of Mexico. Its best states in terms of the 1982 vote were Guanajuato (where it also controls the town of Guanajuato), Tlaxcala, San Luis Potosí, Michoacán, and Jalisco. Though it has little potential to be a major challenger to the PRI, it does appear to have considerable "staying power" due to its unofficial ties to the long-standing UNS.

SUCCESS AND SUPPORT OF THE PRI

The purpose of the electoral reforms, especially the most recent one in 1977, and the proliferation of political parties is to give the Mexican political system an aura of liberalization and democratization. One-quarter of the seats in the federal Chamber of Deputies are reserved for the minority parties, and all registered parties are free to compete for the other three-quarters of the deputy seats. The PRI's presidential vote total decreased around 20 percent from 1976 to 1982, giving further indications of greater electoral competition. However, these appearances are quite deceiving, and the PRI continues to dominate the electoral arena and to retain its superior position in the middle of the political spectrum. Its margins of victory in presidential races have ranged from just over two-thirds of the vote in 1982 to near unanimous support in 1934 (see Table 4). The PRI has never lost a senate seat (the only opposition senator, Cruickshank, essentially had his seat given to him) nor a gubernatorial race. And in the Chamber of Deputies the PRI has had to resort to guaranteeing the opposition its seats. Excluding the "party" or proportional representation deputies (for which the PRI cannot compete as the majority party), the PRI has lost a total of 65 deputy races (or 2.2 percent of the total) since 1943 (see Table 5). The most publicized victories by the opposition have occurred at the local level, but again the PRI has lost only a handful of municipalities. Only 2.4 percent of the nation's cities and towns, and only four of the country's 60 largest urban areas are controlled by parties other than the PRI.

Analysis of the strengths and weaknesses of the PRI's electoral support shows that it is strongest precisely where the PAN is weakest and vice versa. Of course, this is not to state that the two parties are evenly balanced. The PRI's strengths are much stronger than those of the PAN, while the PRI's weaknesses are not nearly so weak as the PAN's. In its poorest statewide showing in the 1982 presidential election (in the Federal District, which is roughly equivalent to a state), the PRI still outpolled the PAN by almost 15 percentage points. In a regional breakdown of the 1982 vote, the ruling party did best in the eastern, southeastern, and southern areas of Mexico (see Table 7). It received over 90 percent of the vote in three states: Tabasco in the east, Quintana Roo in the southeast, and Chiapas in the south. Its worst regions were the center and northern parts of the country. The PRI "only" won 56 percent of the vote in the state of Jalisco, 55 percent in México, and 50 percent in Baja California. Its absolute lowest level of support was in the Federal District—the only state or comparable entity where it did not receive a majority of the vote (48.55 percent to be exact). Since these states include some of the largest metropolitan centers in the nation, the PRI's weaknesses in urban areas are its greatest concerns.[20]

The correlations of party vote with measures of urbanization give further indications of the PRI's problems in the cities. The correlation coefficients between the voting percentages for the PRI and three urbanization variables, utilizing the states as the units of analysis, are all highly negative—demonstrating an inverse relationship between the PRI vote and urbanization (see Table 7). Finally, the PRI received around 80 percent of the nonurban vote and only about 65 percent of the urban vote (see Table 8). The lack of a majority in the Federal District was particularly embarrassing and quite troublesome for the dominant party.

Very little survey research has been done on public opinion and party support in Mexico, but the data that are available suggest that the PRI has been quite adept at fostering support for the system it dominates and the presidential leadership it provides. In his research in the early-1970s, Kenneth Coleman found a high level of support for the electoral system in general and the office of the presidency in particular.[21] His respondents were not naive regarding the low esteem of the congress, however, and showed little support for the Mexican legislative branch.

The issue of abstentionism is a crucial aspect of the level of support the PRI enjoys. Oftentimes, the number of nonvoters is as important a measure of dissatisfaction with the PRI as is the vote for the opposition parties. References are frequently made to the "party of abstentionism" as the chief challenger to the PRI, and PRI officials often treat the number of abstentions as seriously as they view the number of votes for the PAN. In one of the most positive signs for the ruling party, the level of abstentionism declined in the 1970s. Though the proportions of abstentions did increase in the 1960s (the abstention rate was 29 percent in 1958, 31 percent in 1964, and 35 percent in 1970), this trend reversed itself in the next decade. The 1976 level of abstention was reduced to 31 percent and fell even further in 1982 to 25 percent. To the PRI, the fact that 75 percent of the registered electorate actually voted in 1982 was more important than the fact that Miguel de la Madrid received some 70 percent of the votes cast for president.

A survey by Roderic A. Camp and Miguel A. Basañez conducted in November of 1982 demonstrated that even in the worst of times the PRI—particularly its presidents of the nation—is still quite popular.[22] The last year of recent *sexenios* has been fairly tumultuous, and this was especially so in 1982. President López Portillo was arguably at his lowest ebb after the devaluations, loan defaults, bank nationalizations, and exchange controls of the last year. Yet, in this 1982 national survey 35 percent of the respondents rated the López Portillo administration overall as very good, 38 percent rated it as satisfactory, and only 21 percent said unsatisfactory. An approval rating of over 70 percent is remarkable, especially given that Mexico was in the midst of a major economic crisis and a minor political crisis. As Camp and Basañez surmised, either the Mexican people have a very high tolerance level for their government and the ruling party or they are afraid to voice their criticisms.

Several common responses are often given by Mexicans when asked why they vote for the PRI. One is a somewhat fatalistic reaction—the PRI is going to win, so why not support the sure victor. Predictions of PRI electoral successes become self-fulfilling prophecies. Another response is essentially that the familiar face of the PRI, even though its performance may be evaluated negatively, is preferable to an unknown alternative (such as the PAN), which could be even worse once in office. Many Mexicans credit the PRI with achieving political and social stability in the past and as the best hope for maintaining this peace in the future. One television commercial used by the PRI in the 1985 elections played upon these sentiments. It first depicted scenes of violence and social upheaval in the Middle East, Central America, and even Europe. It then flashed an image of a child flying a kite in the park and stated that this represented the peace and stability in Mexico that has been produced by the PRI over the last 50 years.

A more recent poll conducted in Mexico City and Monterrey in 1984 did show some negative repercussions of the stiff austerity policies in the early years of the de la Madrid administration.[23] While 26 percent of those surveyed said de la Madrid was achieving his stated goals, 17 percent said he was not, and 52 percent said he was trying to achieve them but failing. Still, the Mexican people appeared surprisingly tolerant. Despite the economic sacrifices being made, very few outward manifestations of this discontent (such as strikes, demonstrations, protests, or forms of political violence) occurred.

The Camp-Basañez poll showed the potential source of opposition to the PRI. While public officials and peasants (two groups very well integrated into the PRI) gave the government its highest levels of support, the greatest signs of disapproval came from students, industrialists, businessmen, and professionals. Combining these data with the results of the most recent elections, they concluded that the urban middle class represented the strongest threat to PRI dominance.[24] The ruling party effectively controls the lower class; and the upper class, which has benefited the most from the national development strategy, recognizes the rewards for cooperating with the PRI. However, the urban middle class remains a source of discontent and opposition to the PRI.

CONTROL AND CO-OPTATION OF OPPOSITION PARTIES

One of the most successful strategies for the PRI in maintaining its political dominance while preserving the stability of the system has been its astute treatment of the minority parties. For decades the leadership of the ruling party has recognized the utility of allowing and sometimes even encouraging opposition parties as instruments for creating legitimacy and providing outlets for criticism, alienation, and frustration. Yet at the same time the PRI hierarchy has not been prepared to tolerate significant victories by the opposition. So, it has attempted to mix co-optation and control in order to achieve a fine balance between using the minority parties to serve the goals of the PRI and preventing them from becoming significant threats to the dominant coalition.

Obviously, co-optation is the preferred strategy because it is a positive-sum game that benefits everyone—up to a point. The difficulty lies in the fact that only a certain amount of rewards or benefits can be distributed before crossing the unacceptable limits of granting too much power to the opposition. Within the acceptable boundaries, co-optation theoretically can be a very attractive situation for both parties. The party granting the rewards does so in the context of some kind of exchange, i.e., receiving in return something it values, such as political support or token opposition. The party accepting the rewards usually is in no position to complain about the minimal nature of the benefits being transferred. In fact, it normally is quite appreciative of the resources it is acquiring, whether those are personal gains, group recognition, or others. Certainly, the Mexican situation provides a number of examples of the co-optation of opposition parties, in which the PRI achieves the legitimizing aspects of a "multiparty" system while the minority parties receive political rewards which otherwise would not be available.

The two classic cases of co-optative politics in the Mexican party system are the PPS and the PARM—the former being a co-opted party on the left of the political spectrum and the latter on the right. Both parties have been noted for their unqualified support for PRI presidential candidates. Even when it ran its own presidential candidate in 1952 (Lombardo Toledano), the PPS was charged with splitting the leftist vote and weakening a potentially popular opposition candidate to the PRI's Ruiz Cortines. After the election the PPS jumped on the Ruiz Cortines bandwagon and has endorsed every PRI presidential candidate since that time. In return for its support at the national level, the PPS has received more local deputies to the federal Chamber than its percentage of the total vote legally entitled it. The most blatant act of co-optation occurred in the mid-1970s when the PPS leader Jorge Cruickshank was granted the only opposition senate seat in Mexican history in return for his collusion with the PRI in nullifying an apparent gubernatorial victory by the PPS. As in this case, the PRI's most successful co-optation often focuses on individual political leaders within the parties.

The PARM was created to be an outlet for old-line military leaders discontented with their new role outside the dominant party in the 1950s. Ruiz Cortines even encouraged the establishment of this opposition party in order to placate the aging generals. In exchange for its consistent support of the PRI's presidential candidate, the PARM has received federal deputies in greater numbers than its voting support warrants. Even the recognition and existence of the PARM is a concession by the ruling party, because it has regularly failed to meet the legal requisites for party registration.

The notion of political co-optation is not limited to the obvious cases of the submissive PPS and PARM. Even the genuinely independent opposition parties (which in 1985 included the PAN, the PSUM, the PRT, the PST, the PMT and the PDM) have been co-opted to a degree. Essentially what these parties have gained is simply the right to participate (which in historically authoritarian Mexico is no small matter) plus a number of fringe benefits. In addition to their legal status, all registered parties receive free office space and equipment as well as equal allotments of free television time. Though these parties do not enjoy representation in excess of their voting support, they are still enticed into the PRI-dominated electoral system by the challenge of being able to compete for elective posts, to win control of some municipalities, to gain representation in state and national legislative branches, and to present their party platform and ideology to the Mexican people.

From the perspective of the PRI, the benefits from the participation of these opposition parties are even greater than those from the inclusion of the PPS and the PARM. The latter two parties are universally recognized as puppets for the dominant party, and a system that included only these two parties in the so-called opposition would not be deemed competitve by even the most naive observer. However, the PAN, the PSUM, and the others are widely, and correctly, interpreted as truly independent parties representing real alternatives to the PRI. The legitimacy acquired through their participation is much more significant internationally and domestically. Though one could say that these parties win only as many electoral victories as the PRI will allow them, their inclusion is still perceived as allowing genuine alternative parties and philosophies to compete freely (if not fairly) for political power. The disadvantages for these parties (the reasons why they cannot compete on an equal basis with the PRI) are fairly subtle, so their participation greatly enhances the democratic image of the Mexican system.

As noted earlier, the issue of participation has been particularly vexing for the PAN. Soon after creating the ruling party, Calles recognized the need for an institutionalized party of the opposition and the systemic advantages of the existence of such a party. The PAN became this party of the opposition in 1939 and quickly rose to be the major party challenging the PRI. Yet its challenge has never been severe and it, more than any other entity, grants legitimacy to the Mexican regime. This notion of actually supporting the PRI and its system by serving as the opposition has not escaped the leadership of the PAN. On a number of occasions, especially national conventions preceding presidential elections, the PAN has openly debated whether abstention (thereby removing the legitimizing factor) or participation was the best means of opposing the PRI. In the postwar period the PAN has almost always chosen participation. Thus, in a fashion it has always been co-opted by agreeing to provide the PRI with a "loyal opposition" while resigning itself to a guaranteed defeat, at least in the race for true national power.

The other strategy utilized in the PRI's approach to the opposition is control. Though not preferable to co-optation in an ideal situation, realistically it is probably employed more frequently and more effectively. Actually, its potential costs for the ruling party are greater, in terms of lost international prestige, commitment of greater economic resources, and the destabilization associated with increased alienation. But whereas the strategy of co-optation has obvious limits (the dominant party can share only so much power), the strategy of control is essentially limited only by the political will of the PRI.

The most obvious, yet least brutal, instrument for electoral control is the Federal Election Commission (CFE). Though the CFE is no longer monopolized by the PRI, the ruling party still dominates its decision-making through the minister of *gobernación*, a presidential appointee who chairs the CFE. Clearly, the opposition parties are now in a better position to affect the decisions of the CFE (for the 1982 elections the Commission included fifteen voting members, of which eight were the representatives of each of the registered opposition parties). However, the necessary unity has generally not been achieved by the minority parties in the CFE, and the PRI has continued to dominate its proceedings. This control over the chief electoral body has allowed the PRI to perpetuate two very effective measures in repressing the opposition: denial of registration and annulment of elections. The best exammples of legal registration being denied opposition parties are the PCM from 1946 to 1978, the various political wings of the UNS in the postwar period, and the PMT in 1981. The examples of opposition electoral victories being annulled by PRI-dominated bodies are numerous, but among the most cited cases are gubernatorial and mayoral races in Baja California and the Yucatán in the late-1960s and more recent municipal elections in Cuidad Obregón and Juchitán.

Whereas the CFE provides an administrative check on the minority parties, a number of other strategies utilize more covert and indirect (and often extralegal) means of control. Though it is difficult to specify the PRI explicity as a causal factor, a divide-and-rule scenario is clearly applicable to the multiplicity of minority parties, especially those on the left. Even if it is not directly responsible, the PRI certainly has benefited from and at least has encouraged the proliferation of leftist parties, their interparty conflicts, and their inability to unite around a single presidential candidate.

Other, more serious, tactics employed by the PRI and its agents have included arrests, harassments, and intimidation of opposition leaders. The PCM prior to 1978 was particularly plagued with arrests of its members, and in a more recent case a prominant *panista* in Sonora, Adalberto Rosas López, was charged with contempt by the state legislature. Rosas López was the outgoing major of Cuidad Obregón whom the state legislature accused of delaying the vote count in the 1982 election for his successor. The Sonoran legislature overturned the results of that election (thus allowing the PRI to win) and filed the contempt charges against Rosas López.

Another form of harassment against opposition leaders has been to withhold crucial government services and funds from municipalities under the control of opposition politicians. These deprivations are intended as a form of punishment for any citizenry that dare reject the PRI and intimidation for others that might do so in the future. Recent examples in which the PRI has been able to deny funds to an opposition mayor include a number of the northern cities under PAN control, and, of course, Juchitán under the PSUM affiliate. In fact, Juchitán is almost a textbook case in which various forms of harassment, the overturning of elections, and violence have been used against the opposition. First, funds were denied, and the local radio station was even jammed by a federal transmitter. These actions were followed by violence between partisans of both sides, the annulment of the first elections, and allegations of fraud against the PRI in the special elections that, of course, brought the PRI back to power. Finally, the leftists had to be forcefully removed by the military. Of course, examples of violence against the opposition have not been limited to forceful evictions from city halls. In 1983 at least one municipal official and several political activists from opposition parties were killed in incidents in Chiapas, Puebla, and Guerrero.[25] The opposition blamed the PRI, which, obviously, denied the accusations.

The final means utilized by the PRI to control and manipulate the opposition parties, as well as the electoral process, are corruption and fraud. Admittedly, social scientists, including this author, are often wary of reaching firm conclusions regarding the impact of fraudulent electoral practices, because we have no valid or reliable measures of the phenomenon. However, the employment in Mexico of a variety of methods of illicitly altering the results of elections is undeniable. For example, one of the most widely accepted charges is that the legal requirement that voting results not be released until one week after the polls had closed was designed to allow the PRI ample time to manipulate the results of that election. As Daniel Levy and Gabriel Székely so aptly summarized the situation: "That many of the electoral results have been based on fraud, as is often charged, is almost uncontestable, although we may never know the specifics of each case."[26] Nor will we probably ever know the extent of the electoral fraud. Our data on the degree to which elections are manipulated by the PRI consist primarily of opposition charges of deception in elections and of a few case studies of political corruption.[27]

Interestingly enough, some reputable news sources in recent years have carried stories quoting government and party officials regarding the extralegal alteration of electoral results by the PRI. Specifically, unnamed officials within the ruling party and also within the federal government have admitted that electoral fraud and rigged elections were employed by the PRI in the fall 1983 elections in Baja California. The president of the PRI, Adolfo Lugo Verduzco, was even quoted by name as admitting that some party leaders have been "corrupt."[28] Though one should be skeptical of accusations that the PRI is in power solely through the stealing of elections, certainly illicit manipulation of electoral results by the PRI has been used in several cases as a last resort to insure its victory at the polls.

FUTURE ELECTORAL CHALLENGES TO THE PRI

Though the PRI is not about to lose its electoral grip on the nation's political system, in the mid-1980s it certainly faced the greatest electoral challenges in its history. The elections in 1982 and 1983 provided the first glimpse of a deterioration in the PRI's electoral base. Miguel de la Madrid polled a lower proportion of the total vote than any previous PRI candidate, and the ruling party was exposed as never before in having glaring weaknesses among the urban middle class and in the northern and central states. The 1983 state and local elections, which may have been the most honest ever, brought the PRI its greatest set-backs in municipal races, with twelve northern cities lost to the opposition. Though the PRI rebounded in 1984 and claimed victory in 35 out of 38 municipalities being contested in Coahuila, the political costs were substantial. The charges of fraud were more frequent and vehement than ever before, and surprisingly violent protests broke out in a number of cities. Some survey research indicated that the austerity program of de la Madrid in the early 1980s had noticeably reduced popular support for the PRI, which received almost 5 percent less of the vote for federal deputies in 1985 than in 1982.

The PAN obviously presents the greatest threat to the dominance of the PRI. Though the PDM has a stronghold in Guanajuato and the PSUM has received much publicity (especially regarding the case of Juchitán), only the PAN is capable of mounting a widespread and serious electoral challenge to the PRI. In 1985 both sides viewed the July elections for the 400 seats in the federal Chamber of Deputies, seven gubernatorial openings, deputies in six states, and municipal posts in two states as potentially a pivotal turning point in Mexican electoral history. Specifically, the PAN hoped for gubernatorial victories in two northern states: Nuevo León and Sonora.

In Nuevo León the PAN had chosen an outstanding businessman, Fernando Canales Clariond, as its candidate; and the PRI responded by running Jorge Alberto Treviño Martínez, a respected young lawyer. Though his reputation as a *técnico* was not considered an asset, Treviño Martínez was believed to be a wise choice for the PRI with a good chance of retaining the party's control in that state. The PAN was thought to have a better opportunity to unseat the PRI in Sonora, where the PAN candidate was Adalberto Rosas López, a well-known agronomist by profession and former mayor of Ciudad Obregón. As mentioned earlier, Rosas López had a history of standing up to the PRI. The hopes of the ruling party were in the candidacy of Rodolfo Félix Váldez, whose principal political experience was as the minister of transportation and communications in the early years of the de la Madrid administration. A victory by the PAN in either state would certainly have been without precedent, as the PRI has never lost a gubernatorial election and views these positions as crucial to maintaining political control.

On the one hand, the results of these elections produced a sweeping victory for the PRI. Canales Clariond and Rosas López were both defeated by wide margins, as the PRI won all the gubernatorial races and 290 of the 300 "majority" federal deputies. On the other hand, the elections were a serious setback to efforts by some within the Party to reform its structure and liberalize the electoral system. Scores of foreign journalists documented numerous cases of electoral fraud in probably the most closely watched elections in Mexican history. PAN poll watchers were refused certification and harassed at many polling places. Reporters observed PRI supporters tampering with ballot boxes before and after the voting. Fictitious names were discovered on voting rolls, and many opposition members were purged from the rolls. Though the 1985 elections probably were not the most fraudulent in Mexican history, they severely damaged the democratic image of the PRI and actually reduced the popular support that the Party had been carefully cultivating through its liberalization efforts.

5

Internal Organization of the PRI and Interest Group Incorporation

Political parties are said to perform four chief functions: interest representation, interest mobilization, conflict resolution, and education. First, interest representation implies that the citizenry have already formulated specific opinions and interests and simply need a conduit through which to communicate their concerns to the decision-makers. Political parties then serve as that channel for representing interests that flow from "the bottom up." Second, interest mobilization suggests that parties, having their own political interests, mobilize support for their platform and their candidates. The parties still serve as a link between the masses and the elites; however, the implication here is that the parties have the responsibility to generate support among an otherwise apathetic population. Hence, the flow of political communications in this functional area is from "the top down." A third function involves conflict resolution or the simplification of choices. Political parties are the instruments through which political differences are resolved. They provide the choices (candidates and policy preferences), contest elections, and allow the voters to decide the outcome. Even one-party systems fulfill this role of resolving conflict, as competition occurs within the party and political choices are simplified to the extreme. Finally, political parties serve an educational function by stating issues and presenting arguments. Of course, they are also providing political propaganda designed to influence public opinion.

Each of these functions is performed to varying degrees in all party systems. Thus, the Mexican PRI is not unique in emphasizing one or two functions over others. For example, the PRI has a very important responsibility for interest mobilization but does little in terms of interest representation. The ruling party in Mexico carries a significant burden for generating support for itself, for the "revolutionary" state, and even for the opposition parties. Since the other parties are so important in legitimizing the system, the PRI has often encouraged them and has influenced the government to guarantee them representation and to provide them with certain resources (office space, media access, etc.).

Another important function for the PRI is the dissemination of propaganda. One of the most significant building blocks of the benignly authoritarian state has been the ability to perpetuate the myth of the Mexican Revolution. Political symbols play a very crucial role in Mexico, and probably the most common symbol is the long-standing association of the Revolution with the "Party of the Revolution" (the PRI) and the "Government of the Revolution," for which the PRI in part provides the leadership. Through its slogans, political campaigns, literature, rallies, posters and billboards, speeches, and other means of political socialization at its disposal, the PRI propagates the myth that the "Mexican Revolution lives on" and that its ideals are personified in the ruling party and in the party's representatives within the government.

The final function fulfilled by the PRI is the resolution of conflict. Though generally well hidden from the eyes of the public (including journalists and scholars), the most important political competition in Mexico occurs within the dominant party. This intraparty competition certainly does simplify the political choices facing the electorate. In reality any real alternatives are eliminated, and the Party nominates candidates that are dutifully rubber-stamped with their approval by the voters. In addition to candidate selection, a host of other political demands and policy choices are addressed within the party apparatus. The only general function of political parties that is largely irrelevant to the PRI is that of interest representation, since by design the populace remains relatively apathetic.

It is instructive to compare the aforementioned functions with the stated "functions and fundamental objectives" that the PRI outlines in Article 1 of its Statutes.[1] Not surprisingly, in the introductory paragraph the PRI says that its principles are identical to the postulates of the Mexican Revolution. Then, the PRI goes on to state the following five objectives: (1) to achieve political power through democratic procedures; (2) to create political, economic, and social conditions more favorable to the "revolutionary uplifting" of the popular sectors; (3) to promote a democratic system of government; (4) to defend national sovereignty and to promote "independent" economic development; and (5) to organize and mobilize the popular and democratic forces of the nation in order to advance, through a "nationalistic, revolutionary" path, the building of an egalitarian society. Obviously, the "educational" function is not made explicit. However, the use of revolutionary symbols is widespread, and the propaganda goal of equating the PRI with revolutionary principles is evident even in these objectives. Interest mobilization is rather openly admitted in the PRI's fifth objective, and conflict resolution (contesting and winning elections) essentially is the topic of the first objective. Thus, even in its own, self-serving, statements of functions, its goals of mobilization, education, and resolving political conflict are evident.

The primary means and most basic strategies for achieving these objectives have been to incorporate the majority of the salient political interest groups into the ruling party and to maintain control over these groups through a hierarchical structure of organization without resorting to much repression. This chapter will first examine the internal organization of the PRI and then discuss the relevant interest groups that have been subsumed under the party's umbrella.

INTERNAL ORGANIZATION

The PRI is formally organized around nine decision-making bodies: the National Assembly, the National Council, the National Executive Committee, the State Assemblies and the Assembly of the Federal District, the State Directive Committees and the Directive Committee of the Federal District, the Municipal Assemblies and the District Assemblies of the Federal District, the Municipal Committees and the District Committees of the Federal District, the Sectional Assemblies, and the Sectional Committees.[2] Though complex in appearances, the PRI's organizational chart is a very centralized structure that has evolved over the years primarily by incorporating most of the major political sectors through functional, regional, and electoral divisions.

Theoretically at least, the supreme organ of the Party is the National Assembly, which meets at least once every six years and is roughly parallel to the quadrennial national conventions of the major political parties in the United States. It is comprised of the National Executive Committee, representatives of the three functional sectors of the Party, the presidents and secretary-generals of the State Directive Committees, and other delegates as determined by the convocation announcement, which is issued by the National Executive Committee.[3] Its most important power is the election of the president and secretary-general of the National Executive Committee, but its prerogatives also include analyzing the national situation and formulating appropriate plans of action for the Party; approving the Basic Plan of Government prior to a presidential campaign (essentially the party platform); and ratifying reforms to the Declaration of Principles, the Program of Action, and the Statutes of the Party.

In reality, the PRI's National Assembly is even less powerful than the national conventions of U.S. parties, because it does not nominate candidates to elective offices. This task is usually accomplished by separate conventions. The National Assembly meets only to approve automatically the decision of the National Executive Committee and to publicize these decisions to the Party's members and to the rest of the nation.

The second national organ of the PRI is the National Council, which meets annually in September or at other times as determined by the National Executive Committee. Much smaller than the National Assembly, its membership includes the president and secretary-general of the National Executive Committee, at least 60 representatives of each of the three functional sectors, and the presidents of the State Directive Committees. The Council's role is partially to serve as a surrogate for the National Assembly when the latter is not in session. The specific powers of the National Council include hearing the annual report of the National Executive Committee, filling vacancies in the posts of president or secretary-general of the National Executive Committee, and reviewing any sanctions imposed on party members by the National Executive Committee. By assigning votes only to functional and regional delegates, the Council is designed to represent only those groups within the Party, whereas the National Assembly has a somewhat more popular (or individual) representation, especially through the unaffiliated delegates that may be chosen.

Though not explicitly stated in Party Statutes, the real source of authority within the PRI is the National Executive Committee (Comité Ejecutivo Nacional, or CEN). It is the CEN that gives direction to the Party, makes policy within the Party, determines the ideological positions of the Party, and intervenes in all other bodies of the Party. Though the smallest of the three national organs, the CEN commands a vast bureaucracy that runs the Party's affairs.

The 21 members of the CEN include a president; a secretary-general; a chief administrator; and eighteen additional secretaries heading different divisions within the Party. The "inner circle" of the CEN is composed of the president and secretary-general (elected by the National Assembly); the secretaries of agrarian, labor, and popular activities (designated by the respective functional sectors of the Party); and the two secretaries of political activities and legislative coordination (elected by the Party caucuses in the Chamber of Deputies and the Senate). The remaining members of the CEN are essentially designated by the inner circle.

Despite the official procedures for selecting all of these posts, the president of the Republic essentially determines the composition of the CEN, particularly the two top positions. These Party leaders are always members of the president's political clique and serve at his pleasure. In fact, the dominance of the national president over the Party bureaucracy has increased over the years. Expanding the size of the CEN from eight in 1958 to over twenty today diluted the influence of the sectoral leaders and allowed the president to control the Party more effectively. Also, decisions in 1965 and 1984 against instituting more democratic procedures for choosing Party candidates allowed the president to retain his influence over the Party electoral machinery.

The explicit powers of the CEN include overseeing all the Party organizations; analyzing and reaching conclusions concerning political questions relevant to the Party; formulating the Basic Plan of Government (party platform); proposing reforms to the Declaration of Principles, Program of Action, and Statutes of the Party; convening the National Assembly and the National Council; designating Party representatives to all external political and electoral bodies; and convening District, State, and National Conventions to select candidates for president of the Republic and for National Congress. The CEN has come not only to coordinate the daily activities of the Party but to dominate all decision-making within the Party. All important actions taken by the Party in areas ranging from recruitment to policy statements are decided upon by the CEN. It even controls the implementation of these decisions throughout the Party bureaucracy—theoretically as far down as the local level.

The president of the CEN, often simply referred to as the president of the Party, has been given considerable authority. He calls all meetings of the CEN (which are frequent), presides over these meetings (as well as those of a host of other Party organs), and implements all decisions of the CEN. He also names all Party under secretaries and directors of administrative offices, manages the budget of the CEN, acts on behalf of the CEN in emergencies, establishes any administrative offices deemed necessary, and in general represents the Party externally. Either before or after their tenure with the Party, CEN presidents have at times held high elected or appointed posts in the government (including president of the Republic).[4]

The Party Statutes describe a number of additional Party entities that are directly responsible to the CEN: several "auxiliary organs," three "administrative dependencies," and the Institute for Political, Economic, and Social Studies (IEPES). The auxiliary organs of the CEN are the National Commission of Political Coordination (basically the CEN inner circle), the National Commission of Ideology (designated by the CEN President to analyze the ideological development of the Party), the National Commission of Information and Evaluation (also designated by the CEN president to examine the development of public administration in the country), and Consultative Councils (created whenever necessary by the CEN president to assist the Party in whatever collaborations are required to carry out a specific Party activity). The administrative dependencies are the Office of Juridical Affairs, the Office of Administrative Services, and the Office of Community Development and Family Concerns.

Though one of the newest creations within the Party, the IEPES has assumed a high profile as the PRI's in-house think tank or planning agency. As described in the Party Statutes, the IEPES is the "technical organ of the Party" with responsibilities to "study, investigate, and analyze national and regional problems."[5] It has organized numerous conferences, seminars, and "consultations" bringing together Party leaders, government officials, professionals, and intellectuals. It has been particularly active during presidential campaigns, and in 1981 the IEPES was responsible for writing the party platform for the 1982 electoral campaign.[6] The IEPES presented the platform to the National Assembly in October of 1981 for ratification and over the next eight months organized over 100 public meetings (under the rubric of "popular consultations") to publicize and discuss the PRI's 1982 electoral platform.

The remaining decision-making bodies of the Party are the assemblies and committees organized at the state, municipal, and sectional (electoral district) levels. The State Assemblies meet at least once a year to represent the Party at the state level and to discuss questions relevant to the states. Delegates are chosen by Party members in a manner established by the order convening the Assembly. One of its most important duties is to elect the president and secretary-general of the State Directive Committees. These Committees are the permanent organ of the Party at the state level and meet at least once a month to direct the Party's state activites. They are organized in a manner similar to the CEN, with a president, a secretary-general, and some fifteen secretaries assigned to specific areas.

The Municipal Assemblies meet at least once a year to serve as the representative and deliberative organs of the Party at the municipal level. The delegates to the Assembly are elected from the local affiliates of the three functional sectors of the Party and from the Party members in the electoral districts. The Assembly chooses all the members of the Municipal Committee, which is the CEN counterpart at the municipal level (meeting at least once a month to direct the programs of the Party within the municipality). However, one indication of the problems that the PRI faces among its rank-and-file membership is that only about one-quarter of the Municipal Committees meet regularly.[7] Despite its efforts to provide meaningful services at the local level, the Party apparently has not been successful in convincing many local members that they have a role in the decision-making process.

Finally, the Sectional Assemblies and Sectional Committees are the equivalents of the National Assembly and the CEN at the level of electoral districts. Again, the Assemblies (composed of all Party members in that electoral district) meet at least once a year to represent the Party generally, and the Committees supposedly meet at least once a month to direct Party affairs at this level. Each Sectional Committee is composed of a president, a secretary-general, and some twelve secretaries in specific areas—all of which are chosen by the Municipal Assemblies, with the exceptions of the sectoral secretaries who are designated by the respective Party sectors.

The internal structure of the PRI is summarized in Figure 1, with the arrows indicating who is officially responsible for electing or selecting the various officers and delegates. Superficially, it would appear that the PRI is a very democratic organization in which the national decision-makers are held accountable to the Party membership at large, to the functional sectors of the Party, and to the state and local organs of the Party. However, this organizational chart does not adequately demonstrate the degree of centralization within the Party and the hierarchical control exercised by the CEN and its president. The lines of authority ultimately flow downward from the office of the president of the CEN (who is actually selected by the president of the Republic). The PRI is really an oligarchy, and all power is focused in the National Executive Committee. The remaining organs serve to communicate the decisions of the CEN to the Party rank and file and to extend CEN control to all levels of the Party. Any attempts at democraticizing the PRI, most notably the reforms initiated by CEN president Carlos Madrazo in 1964, have been singularly unsuccessful.

One characteristic of the PRI that is accurately portrayed by Figure 1 is the extensive penetration of the three functional sectors into all levels of the Party. All sectoral members are also Party members, though the latter also recruit some members from other organizations (such as youth groups). The sectors elect delegates to the National Assembly and the National Council, as well as to many state and local Party organs. Probably the sectors' most important links to the Party elite are the three sectoral secretaries that sit on the CEN. These are usually the secretary-generals of the largest affiliate within each sector (or are at least loyal to the secretary-general).

Since the creation of the PRM by Cárdenas in 1938, the labor, agrarian, and popular sectors of the Party have been the centerpieces for the structuring of a corporatist framework in the PRI. That is to say, the sectoral bodies and delegates seldom represent their members in the Party's decision-making councils. Rather they are the chief instruments for the incorporation of most of the efficacious interest groups in Mexico. In his analysis of the Mexican political system, Roger Hansen concluded that the revolutionary coalition headed by the president of the Republic used the PRI to dominate the country in two ways: (1) by winning elections, and (2) by controlling the sectors already included

Figure 1   Internal Organization of the PRI

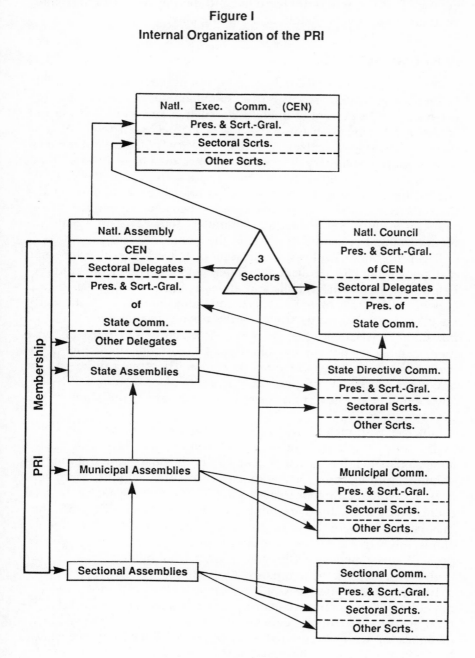

Figure I
Internal Organization of the PRI

within the Party.[8] The former point was discussed in the previous chapter. This chapter will now turn to the latter issue by first examining how Party members are recruited and then by analyzing the labor, agrarian, and popular sectors of the ruling party.

PARTY MEMBERSHIP

The PRI claims some 12 million members (its presidential candidate in 1982, de la Madrid, received over 16 million votes). This figure represents about 18 percent of the total population and around 35 percent of the adult population (over the age of eighteen). In terms of how party membership is acutally achieved, the Party's Statutes suggest that membership is voluntary. Theoretically, once they have enlisted, individuals are then assigned to the appropriate sector of the Party. To be eligible for leadership posts, one has to have been a member of the Party for two years in order to serve on a Sectional Committee, three years for a Municipal or District Committee, four years for a State Directive Committee, and five years for the CEN.

This procedure of voluntary affiliation does work in reality for some members of the PRI, particularly military personnel and large entrepreneurs who join as individuals and are assigned to the popular sector. However, the bulk of the so-called individual members of the Party have achieved that status automatically upon affiliation with a PRI labor union, peasant league, or other association. And most of these memberships are not strictly voluntary. All *ejidatarios* are de jure members of the Party—they are given no choice. The same can be said for any urban workers whose jobs automatically place them in a PRI-affiliated union or any government employees who are by definition FSTSE members.

Linkages with major interest groups have provided the Party with a built-in or guaranteed membership. Of course, they have also created anomalous situations in which many PRI "members" are not only involuntary and inactive Party associates but actually identify with, support, and vote for another party. And in terms of exaggerating the total count, many individuals are duplicate members of the PRI, since they may belong to more than one group affiliated with the Party. One example might be a doctor or a lawyer working for an *ejido*, who by profession is a member of the popular sector but by location in an *ejido* is also a member of the agrarian sector.

To expand its appeal beyond the three traditional sectors, the National Executive Committee over the years has created particular organizations to attract other segments of the population. To maintain its identification with a group that is actually a long-time Party mainstay—the military—the CEN has established the National Commission for

Honor and Justice and the Secretary for Revolutionary Unity. And to reach out to new recruits, a National Council for the Participation of Women and a national youth organization have become active participants in Party affairs. The youth groups on the university campuses have been one of the most promising recruitment mechanisms for new Party leaders. Finally, the CEN has included a Secretary for the Promotion of Sports to provide a recreational service for present members, to encourage sports activities nationwide, and to attract new members with these sorts of interests.

Beyond the creation of these new affiliates, the PRI has been able to escape the stigma of being an exclusively passive organization (relying upon a guaranteed clientele) only by emphasizing the provision of crucial services. Traditional theories of organizational behavior conclude that any effective political organization must fulfill service or technical functions in addition to responding to the political demands of its membership.[9] The PRI has taken this role very seriously and has attempted to make Party membership a very attractive and profitable proposition. The PRI has assumed the responsibility of securing critical health, educational, and other social services from the government—if not literally acting as if it were the government.

Previous chapters have alluded to many of the services provided by the PRI. In the first place, a myriad of jobs are available only through the Party. Thus, it can be an abundant source of the most essential ingredient to maintaining even a subsistence standard of living. The Party itself employs tens of thousands of people in its offices and affiliates nationwide. It also can be a necessary and sufficient means for achieving employment in the governmental sector. And, finally, through its unions it controls many jobs in private-sector as well as state-owned industries. Second, in the agricultural sector the PRI has substantial powers to either grant or deny access to crucial resources, from the land itself to the seeds for planting. The peasants most loyal to the Party will be the ones most blessed in terms of acquiring these scarce resources. In a third area, if one has political aspirations for any elective post, the PRI is about the only game in town. The PAN has made some gains under the political reform, but a political pragmatist looking for the most assured means for electoral success will always settle on the PRI. Besides dominating the elective positions, the official party has patronage powers at the local, state, and national levels.

Beyond jobs, agricultural resources, and elective posts, the PRI at the grass-roots level offers a host of its own social services as well as assistance in soliciting other services from the state.[10] The PRI's district office is frequently the center of many neighborhood activities. Vocational classes are often given in such fundamental areas as sewing, cooking, and typing. In some regions, the Party even provides officially recognized educational programs. Furthermore, its affiliated groups may supplement state medical aid with their own health care programs. And the most blatant efforts by the Party to build support through providing goods and services involve the free distribution of food, from staples like rice and beans to candy.

Probably more important than its own services are the Party's abilities to secure government provisions. Though it has not been very successful at organizing Municipal Committees, the PRI has been quite adept at soliciting municipal services from local authorities. In fact, from the viewpoint of the local resident the distinction between the official party and the local government may be quite blurred—a confusion that Party officials do not discourage. If a neighborhood wants to inquire regarding its water, sanitation, electric, or other city services, the local PRI office may be its first and last stop. The PRI officials then represent the residents in presenting their pleas before the appropriate government bodies, which more than likely are staffed by loyal *priistas*.

Besides generating loyalty and support and recruiting more members, these service functions gain the PRI immediate benefits in terms of being able to mobilize its local or affiliated patrons for rallies, public celebrations, and any other mass displays of public opinion. One of the most notorious characteristics of Mexican politics is the PRI's ability to produce massive crowds at its political gatherings. Media reports of one-half million or more participants at a May Day parade, a presidential campaign rally, or a demonstration in support of a monumental decision (the 1982 bank nationalization being a case in point) are not exaggerated. However, the lack of spontaneity and voluntary spirit in the huge throngs is evident to even a casual observer. Scattered throughout the crowd will be clusters of participants who are signing lists, turning in cards, or otherwise having their attendance recorded. The precise incentives for their presence (or disincentives for their absence) will vary, but either some significant reward (cash bonus, for instance) is offered for their attendance or a serious penalty (loss of one day's pay possibly) is exacted for their absence. In addition, the participants are transported to the site in government and Party trucks (the distinctions between the two institutions at such events are negligible); are often provided food and drink by the event's sponsors; and are given banners, hats, placards, and other political paraphernalia trumpeting the Party's cause. In some instances, the PRI's manipulation of its affiliates goes beyond a single, one-day demonstration. For example, in the *Excélsior* case the PRI recruited peasants to engage in a long-term land invasion in order to pressure and embarrass the newspaper.

Thus, the PRI's linkages to its rank-and-file members are extensive but not strong, at least in terms of ideological motivations or personal bonds. Membership, recruitment, and participation in Party affairs are generally not voluntary and sincere forms of political behavior. Membership is primarily automatic and guaranteed (achieved through the affiliated groups); recruitment is accomplished through material incentives (not identification with an ideology or even charismatic leaders); and participation is also encouraged through pecuniary measures.

THE LABOR SECTOR

Even before the creation of the ruling party and its functional sectors, organized labor in Mexico was frequently co-opted and controlled by the state. The first important labor organization was the Casa del Obrero Mundial, founded in 1912 primarily by anarcho-syndicalists. After being repressed under both Madero and Huerta, Carranza's ally General Obregón recognized the potential political power of the Casa, donated a new building for its headquarters, named the young labor leader Luis Morones as its general manager, and even made a hefty financial contribution to the Casa. In February of 1915 the Casa signed the first formal labor-government pact with Carranza. In return for organizing privileges granted by the state, the Casa provided Carranza and Obregón with the Red Battalions, made up almost entirely of workers from Mexico City and the state of Veracruz, to fight against the peasant followers of Villa and Zapata.

The Constitution of 1917 (Article 123) granted labor many pathbreaking benefits, from an eight-hour day to extensive organizing rights. However, all these rewards still could be withheld by the state, which clearly retained the upper hand vis-à-vis organized labor.[11] Labor disputes were settled by arbitration boards, and whenever the labor and management representatives on the board disagreed, the government delegate held the deciding vote. The state could also declare any labor actions illegal and repress them. Legal status for a recalcitrant union could be denied or revoked by the government. And labor was constitutionally limited to address only pecuniary issues relevant to the workers and could not act upon broader political questions.[12]

The Casa's relationship with Carranza had deteriorated, and in 1918 he collaborated with Morones to form the CROM as a pro-government and pro-capitalist labor confederation. Until 1928 the CROM enjoyed extemely close ties to the Obregón and Calles administrations. In exchange for helping weaken more independent unions, such as the electricians and the railroad workers, *Cromistas* were placed in a host of high governmental posts, including federal deputies and senators, several state governors, two cabinet ministers (Morones was labor minister), and a mayor of the Federal District.[13] But Morones and the CROM became discredited in 1928 when Morones flirted with the notion of running against Obregón. The CROM belatedly endorsed Obregón, but the support was too late. By 1929 all government support for the CROM had been withdrawn.

The 1931 Labor Law codified many of the state's powers of control over unions that had been included in Article 123 of the 1917 Constitution. The law was not well received by the labor movement, and one author compares it to the corporatist labor code of Mussolini's Italy.[14] The generous benefits were still available for the unions that would subordinate themselves to the government. But the law contained many restrictions that could be used against any defiant unions. Conditions were stipulated under which both employees and employers groups could legally organize, and illegal unions were prohibited from striking or negotiating contracts. Compulsory unionization and closed shops were prohibited. The government-dominated arbitration boards were codified in the law, as was the government's power to declare a strike illegal and use force to repress it.

Organized labor was officially brought under the umbrella of the ruling party in the 1930s. With Morones discredited, Vicente Lombardo Toledano became the leading figure for the Mexican labor movement. In 1928 Lombardo Toledano had split from the CROM to form the CGOCM, which soon became the largest labor organization in the nation. Both Lombardo Toledano and President Cárdenas wanted to create a single confederation of labor unions, and using the CGOCM as the springboard, they established the CTM in 1935. The initial program of the CTM specifically precluded collaboration with the government; but at the urging of its Central Committee, in 1936 the CTM's first congress emphasized siding with the progressive forces under Cárdenas and his administration. The CTM was rewarded with immediate benefits in terms of government financial aid and a multitude of political appointments. When Cárdenas reorganized the ruling party into the PRM in 1938, labor was one of the four functional sectors that were officially incorporated into the Party and thereby received institutionalized support. Though the CTM with some 600,000 members was the core of the Party's labor sector, the CROM, the Confederación General de Trabajadores (CGT), and the miners and electrical workers unions were also included. Labor certainly was favored under the Cárdenas government, but labor was still subordinate to the interests of the state and, after 1938, to those of the ruling party as well.

The labor sector has continued to be manipulated by the government and by the Party in the postwar period through four strategies. First, a very obvious tactic of divide and rule has been utilized with organized labor. Though the CTM has represented from 70 to 90 percent of the PRI's labor sector, a number of other labor groups outside the CTM have been periodically established and favored so as to weaken labor unity. The first split in labor ranks was the ouster of Lombardo Toledano at the CTM. He had actually supported pulling the CTM out of the PRI. As part of the conservative bent of the 1940s, Avila Camacho had Lombardo Toledano replaced as head of the CTM by Fidel Velásquez, a more moderate and malleable labor figure. Lombardo Toledano then founded a separate labor organization and political party, though neither came to have much clout. Another division within labor ranks occurred when a number of progressive unions quit the CTM to form the Central Unica de Trabajadores, but this attempt at an independent labor organization suffered its own internal conflicts and soon split.

In the early 1950s, Ruiz Cortines helped a number of labor groups create the Revolutionary Confederation of Workers and Peasants (Confederación Revolucionaria de Obreros y Campesinos, or CROC) to rival Velásquez' CTM. Various presidents have wooed both the CROC and the newer version of the CROM whenever they felt the CTM was becoming too strong. For many years the PRI's labor sector was divided between the Block of United Labor (Bloque de Unidad Obrero), which was led by the CTM, and the National Center of Mexican Workers (Central Nacional de Trabajadores Mexicanos), which was a weaker counterweight headed by the CROC. Díaz Ordaz actually pressured them to unite, which they did in 1966 by coming together under the rubric of the Congreso del Trabajo (CT). The CT has remained as the umbrella organization of the PRI's labor sector, bringing together eight labor confederations, seven federations, and nineteen independent unions. However, the labor sector is still the least unified of the three functional groupings within the Party, and the CT is considerably more decentralized than the umbrella organizations for the other sectors. Finally, the greatest division within organized labor is the existence of the powerful and large union for government employees (FSTSE) not only outside the CTM but even outside the PRI's labor sector. The FSTSE has been placed in the Party's "popular" sector in part to provide a counterbalance to the CTM in the labor sector.

The second strategy for subordinating the labor sector has been co-optation.[15] As both incentives and rewards for their docile participation within the confines of the Party, unionized labor (which is only about one-quarter of the total urban labor force) has enjoyed a number of benefits. Individual labor leaders have received a variety of political posts within the Party and within the government. The most frequent Party position acquired by labor leaders has been at the regional level, where 38 percent of the top offices have been held by the labor sector. Within the government, the majority of labor representatives have become federal deputies, but quite a few federal senators and governors are also former labor leaders.[16] The unions themselves have enjoyed an economic subsidy from the state in terms of direct financial contributions. Unions have never been successful at collecting their own dues. As few as 10 percent of union members are estimated to pay any union dues. Thus, the state provides the bulk of organized labor's finances. In the 1970s the government allegedly provided up to several million pesos annually to the unions within the ruling party.[17]

Collectively, unionized workers have gained access to a number of government-sponsored social programs in the areas of education, health, and housing. The 1962 profit-sharing plan and the 1971 public housing program (INFONAVIT) are examples of specific policies that were enacted to reward labor. The profit-sharing decision was part of López Mateos' attempt to move leftward and placate organized labor in the early-1960s; and the INFONAVIT program was a reward to labor for not supporting the demands of the student protestors in 1968.

The third tactic that the state has used to dominate labor organizations has been control. As has been discussed, the government can exercise broad powers over unions through its discretionary authority to grant or deny legal status to unions, to decide the legality or illegality of strikes, and to impose settlements through the government-dominated arbitration boards. Negative legal rulings have often completely suppressed an undesired union group or purged dissident leaders from a union. Examples include denial of legal status to Lombardo Toledano's new confederation on a technicality in 1949 and government maneuvers to remove radical leaders from their posts in the petroleum workers union in 1960.

Extralegal techniques have also been used, such as allowing pro-government workers to intimidate through violence an independent union or blocking dissidents from attending union meetings. Finally, union leaders can be imprisoned, as was the head of the railroad workers union, Demetrio Vallejo, in the 1958–1959 strike. The charge against Vallejo was sedition under the broad Law of Social Dissolution, which enabled the government to equate political dissent with subversive and seditious acts. Vallejo was sentenced in 1963 to sixteen years in prison for "conspiracy and sabotage against the state." International pressure secured his release in 1968, and President Echeverría finally repealed the law under which he had been imprisoned.

Yet another means for insuring the subservience of unions and their members has been corruption.[18] One of the greatest sources for union graft has been the control over jobs. Pro-government union leaders are given authority to dispense jobs, and the union members pay for acquiring the jobs either through their loyalty to the union boss or actual monetary bribes (or both). Of course, one has to join the favored union even to have the opportunity to secure the job. And dissident members can lose their jobs if they are expelled from the union. In a form of bribery at a different level, employers are known to be able to buy labor peace by making payments to union leaders, who in turn can use union funds for personal means so long as they do not challenge government policies.

The petroleum workers union, Sindicato de Trabajadores Petróles de la República de México, (STPRM) is one of the most powerful unions in Mexico, due to its size (about 150,000 members) and its location in such a crucial industry. The STPRM is also widely known as the most corrupt union in Mexico. In addition to its scope and economic importance, the union's power stems from its special relationship with both PEMEX and the government. The union is often favored with wage increases double the average in other industries; and at PEMEX the union controls all jobs, subcontracts 50 percent of all petroleum drilling contracts, and collects a 2 percent commission for "social works" from all outside contractors. The potential for corruption is obviously great under these circumstances. Jobs and contracts are secured only after a payment to the union (allegedly up to $2,000 per job and a 35 percent commission on contracts). Manuel Buendía, the widely read Mexican columnist who was murdered in 1984, estimated that union leaders netted $750 million annually from their legal and illegal activities.[19] Of course, petroleum graft has served a purpose beyond enriching a few leaders. A powerful union, which had been quite militant in the days before Cárdenas' nationalization of the petroleum companies, has become one of the most loyal and important supporters of the PRI.

In addition to the financial graft, many stories have circulated about petroleum union thugs beating, kidnapping, and even killing union dissidents opposed to the rule of Salvador Barragán Camacho, secretary-general of the union and also a federal senator, and Joaquín Hernández Galícia (commonly known by the nickname "La Quina"), the behind-the-scenes godfather of the union. At least two dissidents were murdered in 1983, and even past secretary-generals who wavered in their support of La Quina have been killed. Also in 1983, after accusations by Barragán Camacho and Hernández Galícia, a lower-level union boss (Héctor García Hernández) was charged with stealing $6.6 million in union funds. Not surprisingly, García Hernández had to be kidnapped by union thugs in McAllen, Texas, before being handed over to the Mexican authorities. He in turn charged his accusers with even greater graft; and though the former director of PEMEX (Jorge Díaz Serrano) was arrested for defrauding the government of $34 million in one transaction, a frequent comment in Mexico was that President de la Madrid's campaign against corruption could only be taken seriously if Barragán Camacho and La Quina were also included in the official corruption charges.

It has been said that Mexico is second only to Argentina as the most unionized nation in Latin America.[20] Some 15 percent of the active labor force and about 25 percent of the urban labor force have been organized into unions. The membership of the CTM alone is estimated at between 1.5 and 3.5 million workers. Although organized labor in Mexico is large, it is not a powerful political force similar to the Peronists in Argentina. Mexican labor unions, almost all of which are incorporated in the PRI, tend to be relatively conservative, oligarchic, and quite loyal to the Party and to the government.

THE AGRARIAN SECTOR

In the formative years of peasant organizations, these agrarian leagues were relatively independent of state control. However, after the creation of the functional sectors within the PRM, the agrarian sector became the most compliant member of the Party's coalition. Ever since the days of Madero and Carranza, with the striking exception of the Cárdenas administration, peasant demands have been the easiest to ignore. Agrarian workers, small farmers, and the indigenous peoples in the countryside have benefited the least from the development strategy of postrevolutionary Mexico. The few examples of policies of direct benefit to the peasantry are quite dated, and more recent overtures to the rural population contain much symbolism but little substance. The most concrete initiative favoring the peasantry occurred almost 50 years ago (the agrarian reform of Cárdenas), and the most important state institutions of today that are relevant to the peasant class are purely cultural attempts to glorify the contributions of the rural and indigenous populations. These institutions are the internationally renowned Ballet Folklórico dance troupe and the National Museum of Anthropology, both located in Mexico City. Through them the modern Mexican state has done an excellent job of preserving rural culture for the edification of urbanites, but it has done a poor job of raising the standard of living of those who still subsist in the countryside (or even of those who have migrated to the cities in search of better opportunities).

Despite having garnered few rewards, the peasant class provides the strongest and most consistent support for the ruling party. Though no figures are exact, the most objective estimates place the PRI's agrarian sector as the largest of the three coalition partners with from 100,000 to 500,000 more members than the labor sector.[21] The goal of the PRI has been to organize every peasant and agricultural worker (and even spouses) in the country, and one author states that the PRI's claim of having enlisted 98 percent of the adult rural population is not totally unbelievable.[22] Finally, as demonstrated in chapter 4, the PRI receives its strongest electoral support in those states with the heaviest concentration of rural voters. While the urban middle class has become the weakest demographic group for the ruling party, the rural lower class has continued as its strongest supporter.

The history of peasant organizations in Mexico has been characterized by two factors: (1) the determination of the ruling coalition to maintain separate identities for urban and rural labor; and (2) a growing intolerance of any attempts by peasants to establish any autonomy from the dominant party. Ever since Carranza enlisted the Red Battalions of urban workers to help defeat the peasant armies, efforts to unify urban labor and the rural peasantry in a common organizational framework have been stymied by the Party establishment. Partly as a result, independent rural unions have been co-opted or repressed more effectively than their urban union counterparts, especially in the postwar period.

The earliest peasant political organization was the PNA, established in 1920 by some followers of Zapata who wanted to support Obregón. This party ushered in what one author labels an "organizing boom" in the 1920s.[23] In the early 1920s a number of peasant leagues (Ligas de Comunidades Agrarias) were created, particularly in the states of Veracruz, Michoacán, and Tamaulipas. The first National Agrarian Confederation was founded in 1923 by peasants that split from the PNA, and the first National Agrarian Congress was held in that same year. In 1926 the various peasant leagues coalesced into the National Peasant League (Liga Nacional Campesina), which claimed 300,000 members by the end of the decade.[24] These efforts at organizing peasants were assisted by several top government leaders in the 1920s (including Obregón) and by politicians who later were instrumental in the PNR (such as Portes Gil). However, until the 1930s the peasant groups were largely independent of the state, and in fact the most influential group in the peasant leagues was the Mexican Communist Party.

Lázaro Cárdenas in the 1930s instigated the most serious changes in rural Mexico through the most extensive agrarian reform ever and through the incorporation of the peasant leagues into the ruling party. The emphasis of his land reform was on collectivizing agriculture through the communal *ejido*, but the *ejido* was devised not only as a means of agricultural production but also as a source of institutionalized political support for the dominant coalition. Cárdenas stressed rural unionization that was allied to (or dependent upon) the state, and in 1938 he created the National Peasant Confederation to further these efforts. He had ,ordered the establishment of a League of Agrarian Communities in every state, and 38 leagues and unions of agricultural workers were represented at the first CNC Congress. All these groups, previously affiliated with the CTM, were transferred into the newly created CNC because Cárdenas wanted the state to control the peasant groups rather than having Lombardo Toledano and the CTM dominate them. The

CNC became both the umbrella group for peasant organizations and the agrarian sector of Cárdenas' reorganized PRM.

In contrast to earlier, failed efforts at linking peasants organizationally to the state (notably the National Rural League of the PNR), by the late 1930s peasant groups had been successfully unified under the banner of the ruling party for two reasons: (1) the CNC had the unequivocal support of the state; and (2) the state was pursuing signficant agrarian reform. State involvement in rural organizing was even more extensive than its commitment to unionization among urban workers. Possibly realizing its potential for monopolizing peasant support, the CNC was dedicated to enlisting every peasant and agricultural worker. All *ejidatarios* are automatically members of the CNC (and thereby of the PRI), and the *ejido* commissioner and supervision committee not only represent the peasants before governmental authorities but are also their official link in the CNC. The *ejido* "owners" therefore have became dependent upon the state and have given the PRI almost unquestioned support.[25] Since the peasants have been granted only the right to farm the land—not actual ownership of the land—they are quite vulnerable to political pressures from the state, which controls the land. Peasants also have to depend upon the CNC for access to necessary resources, ranging from financial credit to seeds.

After Cárdenas left office, the agrarian reform slowed considerably (if not halted altogether). Yet the CNC remained the instrument for controlling and mobilizing peasant support for the PRI. As postwar policies changed to stress private properties and larger holdings, the CNC readily acquiesced with little or no discussion of the impact of these changes. Even when changes in agrarian policy supposedly benefited the peasantry, as under the Echeverría administration, the new policies were imposed "from above" with minimal input from those affected.

Since the creation of the CNC, attempts at independently organizing peasants have been either co-opted or more frequently repressed. Corruption and channeling all rewards through the CNC have been the traditional means of co-optation. Repressive measures have ranged from denial of registration to violence and murder. The earliest militant leader was Rubén Jaramillo, who first attempted to expose the extent of corruption in *ejidos* in his home state of Morelos. Thwarted in his legal efforts, he turned to violence to achieve his ends. But Jaramillo was soon co-opted by the granting of amnesty and the opportunity to work with other progressives in a leftist umbrella organization headed by ex-president Cárdenas. Again frustrated by the lack of progress in his demands for more land reform, he returned to the extralegal avenues in 1961 by leading a land invasion by some 5,000 peasants in Morelos. He was finally killed by the army in 1962. Though his murder tarnished the leftist image of López Mateos, his movement was effectively suppressed.

The Marxist labor leader Lombardo Toledano always wanted to organize workers in the countryside as well as in the city. But Cárdenas created the CNC partly to remove peasants' unions from the dominion of Lombardo Toledano and the CTM. When Lombardo Toledano left the CTM in the late 1940s, he created the General Union of Workers and Peasants of Mexico (Unión General de Obreros y Campesinos de México, or UGOCM), with about 60 percent of its 300,000 members being peasants.[26] However, the UGOCM was denied official recognition by the government and, though it continued to exist, was greatly limited in any legal efforts to represent peasants. Thus, its most successful actions were land invasions, particularly in the northwest, which occasionally resulted in the distribution of the land to the peasants (and at other times produced the physical removal of the peasants by the army). Wearied by its inability to accomplish much from outside the ruling party, in the early 1970s the remnants of the original UGOCM (now labeled the UGOCM–"Jacinto López") officially enlisted in the agrarian sector of the PRI alongside the larger and dominant CNC.

The most recent attempt at creating an autonomous organization was the formation in 1961 of the Independent Peasant Confederation (Confederación Campesina Independiente, or CCI) by some 35,000 peasants from twelve different groups. Within two years, however, it had split between radicals and those still close to the PRI. The more moderate wing of the CCI officially joined the PRI in 1974, so that today the agrarian sector of the Party is composed of the CNC (which includes 23 peasant groups), the moderate CCI (now the Central Campesina Independiente), the UGOCM–"Jacinto López," and the Consejo Agrarista Mexicano.

With all the independent organizations either suppressed or co-opted, radical opponents of the regime's agrarian policies have turned to extralegal or more violent alternatives. The most frequent illegal actions have been land invasions, which have continued at relatively high rates over the last decade or so. For example, even in the midst of the sympathetic Echeverría administration, some reports cited as many as 200 invasions annually.[27] Sometimes the CNC and the Agrarian Ministry have viewed the invasions with empathy and have moved to co-opt them, but on other occasions the army has been called in to repress these illegal actions.

The most militant response has been the outbreak of guerilla violence, especially in the state of Guerrero. In the late 1960s rural guerrillas in the hills of Guerrero, under the leadership of Genaro Vázquez Rojas, carried out kidnappings and even attacks on army garrisons to further their goal of a second Mexican revolution. In 1970 Vázquez Rojas led his followers into an alliance with their urban counterparts, many of whom had been radicalized in the 1968 student movement. The new group, National Revolutionary Civic Action (Acción Cívica Nacional Revolucionaria, or ACNR), became an umbrella organization for guerrilla activities throughout Mexico.[28] One of its earliest actions was the kidnapping of Jaime Castrejón Díaz, the rector of the University of Guerrero and a wealthy industrialist. He was released only after President Echeverría released a number of political prisoners.

The guerrillas in Guerrero staged a second, more daring, kidnapping in 1974 when they seized Rubén Figueroa, a federal senator and at that time the PRI's nominee for governor of Guerrero. Prior to this kidnapping, Vázquez Rojas had died in what the government claimed was a car accident, and the leadership of the ACNR had passed to Lucio Cabañas. With the seizure of Figueroa, Cabañas had substantially increased the stakes (i.e., a federal senator and future governor) involved in the struggle between the guerrillas and the PRI. Political kidnappings seemed an even greater threat to the stability of Mexico when Echeverría's father-in-law, José Guadalupe Zuno Hernández, was seized shortly thereafter by another band of guerrillas. Both Zuno and Figueroa were released on the same day, allegedly after a tidy ransom was paid. Yet the guerrillas posed no further danger to the regime, and when Cabañas was killed in 1974, whatever challenge the ACNR had represented was gone. The rural guerrillas were no more successful than the peaceful, but militant, independent peasant unions in shaking the hold that the PRI had maintained over rural Mexico.

THE POPULAR SECTOR

The third functional sector of the PRI is what is usually termed the "popular" sector. By most measures, this is the smallest of the three sectors.[29] Its umbrella organization is the youngest in the PRI. It is the most diverse sector and the most difficult to characterize.[30] It is the only sector that has no roots in the revolutionary experience. Contrary to urban labor and the peasantry, the so-called popular sector was not the focal point of any revolutionary principles incorporated in the 1917 Constitution. It is the only sector without a legal code linking it to the government. However, despite all these characterizations that might lead one to conclude that the popular sector is only a junior partner of the more dominant labor and agrarian sectors, in reality the popular sector has become the most powerful element within the PRI. It has garnered the most rewards from the economic policies of the state and has achieved the strongest representation in all levels of government.

The popular sector of the PRI is indeed the broadest of the three functional branches. In terms of socioeconomic distinctions, it comes closest to representing the middle class, both urban and rural (though urban elements are the most influential). A comprehensive listing of its membership would include all government employees (which also takes in teachers), small entrepreneurs (industrialists, merchants, and farmers), artisans, professionals (doctors, lawyers, and engineers), intellectuals, members of cooperative enterprises (but not *ejidatarios*), members of youth groups, members of women's groups, bank employees (now they are also state employees), and members of neighborhood associations. Though its membership is widespread, the popular sector is unique in that one confederation (the CNOP) encompasses all affiliates of the sector. Neither the CTM nor the CNC can make the same claim. Among the more significant member organizations of the CNOP are the FSTSE, the National Confederation of Small Landowners (Confederación Nacional de la Pequeña Propiedad Agrícola), the National Confederation of Small Businessmen (Confederación Nacional de Comerciantes en Pequeño), the National Cooperative Confederation (Confederación Nacional Cooperative de la República Mexicana), the Federation of Small Merchants and Industrialists of the Federal District (Federación del Comercio y la Industria en Pequeño del Distrito Federal), and the National Confederation of Intellectual Workers (Confederación Nacional de Trabajadores Intelectuales).[31] The National Confederation of Small Landowners and the National Cooperative Confederation are the largest in terms of membership in the popular sector, but without question the FSTSE is the heart and soul of the sector.

The FSTSE actually predates the CNOP and in 1938 was the main charter member in the PRM representing the popular sector. The CNOP was created in 1943 to unify and coordinate the growing popular sector. But the FSTSE remained the focal point, and on later occasions even floated the idea of separating into its own sector within the PRI. It was placed in the popular sector rather than in the labor sector partially as another attempt to divide and rule organized labor. But the Party hierarchy does not want the FSTSE to establish a separate sector, fearing it would become too powerful and autonomous in its own right.

Today the FSTSE is composed of some 71 unions and 89 organizations, which still exclusively represent government employees. The most recent research estimates that the FSTSE is the largest single component within organized labor in Mexico—even larger than the CTM— and teachers and other educational workers (organized in the National Union of Educational Workers—Sindicato Nacional de Trabajadores de la Educación—or SNTE) make up almost half the membership of the FSTSE.[32] Especially beginning with the Alemán administration (1946–

1952), both the CNOP and the FSTSE were encouraged and favored by the state and quickly became the most influential elements within the ruling party.

The political significance of the popular sector is due to a variety of factors. One of the most important considerations undoubtedly is the desire on the part of the state to maintain the loyalty of its employees. A disgruntled bureaucarcy can be a very destablizing force, especially in a heavily bureaucratized society like Mexico. This need to keep state employees content then becomes an important source of political leverage for the FSTSE. Second, the popular sector contains the most highly educated and politically astute members of the PRI. The CNOP has been the major source of high-level decision-makers within the government. Finally, the CNOP is the most autonomous sector within the PRI. The lack of a federal law establishing linkages between the popular sector and the state is really an asset. There is no equivalent to the Agrarian Code or the Labor Law governing the middle-class representatives in the CNOP. Whereas the agrarian sector is totaly dependent upon the state for land and the labor sector depends on the state for many jobs and for its rights to organize and to be recognized legally, the popular sector is not asymmetrically beholden to the state for any necessary resources. One might argue that bureaucrats and teachers depend upon the state for their jobs, but as relatively well-trained professionals they provide the state with crucial skills that are not in abundant supply.

These advantages have afforded the popular sector, particularly the FSTSE, with more benefits and greater state representation than any other organized group. In the absence of legislative control, state-sponsored benefits have been used as the incentives to co-opt the government employees. The material and social rewards for the bureaucracy include generous medical, hospitalization, and pharmaceutical assistance; extensive retirement programs; low-rent and low-cost housing; and short-term loans. These programs have been administered through the Institute of Social Security and Social Services for State Employees (Instituto de Seguridad y Servicios Sociales de los Trabajadores del Estado—more commonly known as the ISSSTE), which has become one of the largest federal agencies in Mexico. The FSTSE has also achieved greater representation in high government posts than any other PRI affiliate. More cabinet ministers and members of Congress claim political connections with the CNOP than with any other sector, and most of the union leaders in the cabinet are actually from the FSTSE.[33] One author estimated that in the late 1950s the CNOP's representation in elective governmental posts was double that of any other sector.[34] Thus, the CNOP in general and the FSTSE in particular have enjoyed an interdependent relationship with the state. As the most autonomous and politically influential sector of the PRI, it has provided the state with crucial support and loyalty. The state has reciprocated with the most generous package of social and economic benefits granted to any group.

6

Societal Actors Outside the PRI

Several critical political interest groups and political actors are not officially tied to the ruling party. In order to understand both the stability of the system and the extent of party and state control over society, we need to examine the role of these institutions that are external to the PRI. The three groups to be discussed here are the military, the media, and the private sector.

THE MILITARY

Nineteenth-century Mexico was the prototype of a Latin American nation in which military force was the real determinant of political power. Foreign military intervention, domestic military coups, and internal struggles among regional *caudillos* with personal armies plagued Mexico even through the first two or three decades of this century. However, beginning in the 1920s, Mexico began to bring the military slowly under civilian control, and today Mexico possesses one of the most apolitical armed services in all of Latin America.

Though never very professional in a military sense, until 1940 the army was an important source of political power and social change. For several decades after the destruction of the regular Mexican army in 1914, the new Revolutionary Army provided the political leadership that dominated the state apparatus. Ironically, the depoliticization of the army was accomplished by these former military commanders who became the first generation of leaders of the revolutionary governments. Obregón began the process of taming the military in 1920 through a mix of rewards and some punishments, and by 1940 Cárdenas had completed the task through even more direct measures (such as exiling Calles and many *callista* generals).

Several factors explain the depoliticization of the military in the decades following the Revolution.[1] In the first place, frequent struggles, rebellions, and purges within the military both eliminated many of the traditional military *caudillos* and motivated the survivors to create a system devoid of such infighting over political spoils. By 1929 the plethora of original revolutionary generals was reduced to only five: Calles, Cárdenas, Joaquín Amaro, Saturnino Cedillo, and Juan Andreu Almazán. By 1940 all of these had either been relieved of command (Amaro), exiled (Calles), militarily or politically defeated (Cedillo and Almazán), or had retired of their own volition (Cárdenas). These old-line, politicized generals were being replaced by younger, more professional soldiers more interested in purely military operations than political involvement.

Another factor in the political subordination of the military was the development of other political and paramilitary institutions to rival and eventually dominate the armed services. As early as the Carranza presidency, armed peasants fighting for agrarian reform represented a significant counterweight to the Revolutionary Army. Organized labor also became an important source of political and even military power used by Mexican presidents from Carranza to Cárdenas against the army. Finally, the establishment of the PNR, and later the PRM, as the official party began to bring the military under civilian rule. In fact, the most controversial step vis-à-vis the military in the postrevolutionary era was the creation of the military sector of the PRM in 1938. Critics said this move was actually further politicizing the military, whereas Cárdenas defended it by arguing that within the Party the military could be kept in check. In any case, the military sector was disbanded in 1940, with the military officers that held political posts moving to the popular sector of the ruling party. One report concludes that the military itself had little desire to be so directly tied to politics and thus supported the dissolution of the military sector.[2]

President Cárdenas put the finishing touches on the process of depoliticizing the military, as he insured that he was the last revolutionary general to serve as president. Even as war minister immediately prior to his term as president, Cárdenas had stressed the military professionalism of the troops by establishing the Superior War College. And during his administration, he emphasized the technical training of the armed services and their commitment to purely military functions. He also reduced the political influence of the military by creating two separate ministries in 1939: National Defense (combining the army and air force) and Navy.

Most importantly, Cárdenas purged the army of its most politicized elements, particularly the remaining revolutionary generals. Though General Amaro had reduced the military's size of the federal budget by 11 percent in only three years as war minister under Calles, the conservative Amaro was seen as a threat to the reformist policies of Cárdenas and was removed from his military post in 1935. The following year, Calles was sent into foreign exile after being charged with the responsibility for the bombing of a railroad train. General Cedillo, one of the most powerful military bosses with his private army and large landholdings in the state of San Luis Potosí, recognized that Cárdenas was bent on destroying the independent power bases of the revolutionary generals. In 1938 Cedillo rebelled, but he was quickly defeated and was killed in 1939.

The last, major effort at maintaining the political power of the military was the 1940 presidential candidacy of General Almazán, who was the most senior officer of the military hierarchy and an extremely powerful landowner. Almazán opposed the handpicked candidate of Cárdenas and the PRM, Secretary of War Avila Camacho. Though he had a military background, Avila Camacho was perceived as too bureaucratic by the generals who had participated in the Revolution. Despite the backing of many businessmen, landowners, clerics, and the newly created PAN, Almazán lost to Avila Camacho by an obviously distorted margin of almost twenty to one. When Almazán could not mount a serious military threat to the presidential succession from Cárdenas to Avila Camacho, it was clear that the political power of the revolutionary generals had been crushed.

The depoliticization of the military certainly progressed in the 1940s. Alemán was the first civilian president since Ortiz Rubio, and military representation in other high posts also began to diminish substantially. Between 1929 and 1946 eight military officers held cabinet posts other than the defense ministry, but only one officer has done so since 1946.[3] In 1940 fifteen governorships were held by officers, but after 1964 only one military person served as a state governor. Within the Party, no officer has served in a leadership role since the mid-1960s. Even the strictly military posts have been held by a new generation of more technocratic soldiers. General Cuenca Díaz in 1970 became the first secretary of defense who did not participate in the Revolution. His background, like that of his successors, was more strictly professional, with formal military training lacking in previous secretaries of defense.

A number of tactics have been utilized in the postwar period to maintain military subordination. Every four years the assignments of the top military leaders are rotated, so that no one can establish a permanent base of support. Also, promotions have been handed to those officers most loyal to the political leaders, and less reliable soldiers have been demoted or forced into early retirement. Finally, the military elites have been encouraged to enrich themselves through private graft and profiteering (but not through public, political institutions). Thus, they are rewarded for their service without becoming involved in political corruption.

Though the Mexican military in the postwar period has been a de-politicized, subordinate arm of the civilian regime, various factors in the 1970s and 1980s have enhanced the significance, size, and prestige of the armed forces.[4] This renewed importance of the military stems from a growing concern about both internal and external security. In the domestic sphere, the 1968 student demonstrations were perceived by the regime as a very serious threat, and the military was utilized as the chief means for forcefully restoring order in this instance as well as in other university disturbances. In the countryside, the military played a crucial role in repressing rural guerrillas, especially in the state of Guerrero in the 1970s. This experience was not only valuable to the maintenance of internal order but also to the training of the army in counterinsurgency measures. Troops have also been widely used to squash labor strikes; and with the economic problems of the 1980s increasing the potential for domestic tensions, the military task of controlling discontented popular sectors looms ever larger. Another area of increasing concern both to Mexico and to the United States is the proliferation of the drug trade. Here again the army has assumed a more important part in preventing the production and marketing of illicit drugs. Finally, with the recent political reforms and the challenges of the opposition parties, the role of the armed forces in enforcing the electoral victories of the PRI has acquired a renewed significance.

The Mexican oil boom and the unrest in Central America worked together to increase the salience of the military in external affairs. The oil prosperity created the resources for expanding Mexico's regional leadership, and the unrest in Central America and the Caribbean provided the target for Mexican influence. Despite its open support for the Nicaraguan Revolution and desire for a political solution including the armed opposition in El Salvador, Mexico has become increasingly aware of its own national security objectives. Most of the focus is in southern Mexico—in the state of Chiapas along the Guatemalan border. The existence of some 40,000 Guatemalan refugees in over 80 camps near the border is a constant reminder of the instability south of Mexico's borders. As a consequence, Chiapas has received enormous military attention, with the creation of a second military zone in the state (usually each state comprises only one zone), the naming of a former zone commander as state governor, and the appointment of a recognized expert in counterinsurgency as the new zone commander.

These new worries have brought substantial attention to the Mexican military along with a variety of benefits. In the first place, defense budgets have ballooned (with the military's relative proportion of the gross domestic product as much as doubling in one year). Personnel has also gained tremendously—doubling in size in five years. The standard of living for all soldiers has improved drastically, especially in terms of such benefits as social security and housing. Finally, the military has embarked on an impressive modernization campaign, which includes (1) manufacturing its own German G-3 rifles, DN-III armored vehicles, light trucks, and Olmeca-class patrol boats; and (2) purchasing twelve F5-E jet fighters and two Gearing-class destroyers from the United States, 40 Panhard ERC-90 armored vehicles from France, over 50 Pilatus air-craft from Switzerland, and seven amphibious craft and six Halcon-class frigates from Spain.[5]

Thus, with the substantial role of the military in maintaining domes-tic order for the regime as well as the growing concern about external threats in southern Mexico, the armed forces have become a critical base of support for the ruling coalition. Though the army remains sub-ordinate to the civilian leadership of the state and has no influence in the policy-making process, it is an increasingly significant symbol of the state's authority and guarantor of both internal and external order.

THE MEDIA

Mexico has no official news agency and no government-owned me-dia that monopolize the communications sector. Certainly, the PRI has no legally recognized authority over the dissemination of information throughout the country. In some ways, the Mexican media are surpris-ingly autonomous and free from government interference. On the other hand, a number of mechanisms do exist through which the state and the ruling party can greatly influence broadcasting and the print me-dia.

The principal strategy for constraining freedom of the press has been to rely on the numerous financial prerogatives available to the state. And the primary tool for financial control has been the government-owned Producer and Importer of Paper (Productora e Importadora de Papel, S.A., or PIPSA). PIPSA was established in 1935 to coordinate all Mexican purchases of imported newsprint. The objective was to buy in bulk quantities (presently it imports about 250,000 metric tons a year) and thereby command a better price. As a government corporation (with 60 percent state ownership), it pays no import duty and sells the news-print to its affiliated private publishers at wholesale prices. Without access to PIPSA for its supply of newsprint, a newspaper has to buy inferior newsprint in the open market at considerably higher prices. In essence the government operates a monopoly over the supply of news-print and can tremendously affect the well-being of a newspaper by depriving it of this cheap source of paper. In addition to providing the newsprint, PIPSA also can extend credit to a publisher.

A second source of leverage is government advertising. A multitude of state agencies and PRI affiliates spend huge sums of money on announcements, proclamations, and other forms of political advertisements. These government ads are estimated to account for about 20 percent of total advertising revenues for a typical Mexico City daily newspaper.[6]

Bribery or "public relations fees" are another source of financial clout that the state utilizes to produce favorable reporting. In many cases these are direct payments to reporters (called *el sobre*, literally "the envelope," or *la iguala*, translated "the agreement"), who can receive up to $2,000 monthly in this fashion.[7] In other instances, journalists are provided an additional and quite lucrative job with a government or Party organization. Also, the editors of the paper can literally sell news stories (called *gacetillas*) that may appear anywhere from the front page to the back sections of a paper. These are not labeled advertisements and appear as normal news items. One author quotes prices for news stories ranging from $12 to $29 per column inch (triple the cost of normal ads) and says that the respected Mexico City daily *Excélsior* in the mid-1970s sold its second news story (at least the leading story was not for sale) on the front page for $8,000.[8]

These various financial incentives are one of the major reasons why Mexican journalists have an international reputation for being among the most compliant and co-opted reporters in the world. Overt censorship does not exist because it is not necessary. The government has achieved the cooperation of much of the press without direct intervention. As many journalists will admit, they practice a form of "self-censorship." Even among the most independent reporters, some rules (such as never openly criticizing the incumbent president) are inviolate. Hence, the press has come to play a role of image-builder for the state and for the PRI. As one example of the disproportionate amount of attention given to the ruling party, a study of press coverage of the 1982 election found that over half of the news stories on political parties in the year prior to the election concentrated on the PRI (despite the fact that eight other parties were contesting the presidential race).[9]

Another factor discouraging independent journalists is the secrecy that surrounds the political process in Mexico. Journalists are frequently reduced simply to reporting political speeches of elected officials or government press releases. Even when the press acquires independent information, it is usually reluctant to criticize the "government and party of the Revolution." As a spokesman for *Excélsior* openly admitted, the press in Mexico is in "solidarity" with the government.[10]

Often the government does not have to resort to bribes or newsprint subsidies to accomplish its objectives vis-à-vis the media, due to the pervasive linkages between the state and the communications sector. The privately owned daily newspapers are dominated by large business interests and tend to be conservative and naturally uncritical of the state. Televisa is the dominant broadcasting force, a huge conglomerate that owns all the leading television channels (2, 4, 5, and 8 in Mexico City). It is overwhelmingly conservative (with strong ties to the so-called Monterrey Group) and pro-government. One of its four principal owners is a son of former president Alemán, and the private conglomerate cooperates with the government on a number of projects (including program production and satellite equipment).[11] The state also has direct ownership or investment in a number of crucial media outlets. The state owns minority stock in Televisa and through the government corporation SOMEX has a substantial interest in the García Valseca (*El Sol*) chain of over 30 regional daily papers (which include a number of Echeverría loyalists in management positions).[12] The government publishes one Mexico City daily, *El Nacional*, and acquired television Channel 13 in the mid-1970s.[13] Television Channel 11 is operated by the National Polytechnic Institute, and in the 1970s Echeverría even expanded government ownership in the film industry.

The broadcasting sector in particular has been almost void of independent or critical reporting, in part due to the regulatory control that the state exercises over radio and television.[14] The two government agencies that exercise this control are the Secretariat of Communications and Transportation (SCT) and the General Directorate of Radio, Television, and Cinematography (Dirección General de Radio, Televisión and Cinematografía, or RTC) under the secretariat of *gobernación*. The SCT essentially regulates technical aspects, while the RTC focuses on content questions. The SCT issues licenses for owners and even the on-the-air announcers. The law regulating radio and television states that these media "constitute an activity of public interest; therefore, the state must protect that activity and will be obligated to be vigilant toward the required social function compliance."[15] Licenses can be revoked for broadcasters' actions contrary to the "public interest."

Another important power the state can utilize is the authority to command free air time for "public service announcements." A 1960 law required that stations provide gratis "official time" to the state equaling 30 minutes per day plus additional time as needed for emergency or national security messages. Legislation in 1969 further entitled the state to free "fiscal time" (in lieu of taxes), which has been set at 12.5 percent of the broadcast day, to air programs developed by the RTC. The government does not use all its allotted time, but the potential still exists for considerable government interference in programming.

The final means of government control has been physical harassment and violence, especially directed at independent print media. A number of examples serve to illustrate the kinds of tactics that have been employed. Each of these cases involved the suppression of a leftist newspaper or journalist. Criticism from the political right definitely exists in the print media, but the state is most intolerant of leftist dissidents, who are questioning the revolutionary legitimacy of the state and the Party. Attacks from the right often serve the interests of the regime, as it drapes itself in the cloak of revolutionary symbolism. But criticism from the left exposes the contradictions in the state's claims to represent the ideals of Madero, Zapata, Villa, and other revolutionary heroes.

Probably the most repressive campaign was waged against the weekly *¿Por Qué?*, which operated between 1968 and 1974 as an ultraleftist, antiestablishment, and antigovernment outlet.[16] First PIPSA denied the weekly journal its access to the cheaper and better newsprint available only from the government agency.[17] Then the state stopped advertising in *¿Por Qué?*; and partially due to the poor quality of its newsprint, other advertisers followed suit. Finally, as the editors of *¿Por Qué?* were about to contradict in published stories the government's explanations regarding the Figueroa kidnapping in 1974, the army raided its offices, smashed the presses, and arrested all the staffers.

The most significant case of government harassment of a newspaper was the situation of *Excélsior* in 1976.[18] *Excélsior* has always been one of the top three daily newspapers in all of Mexico, and it began to gain international recognition after 1968 when Julio Scherer García became director of the cooperative that runs the paper. *Excélsior* had developed a well-earned reputation as being the most independent, least corrupt, and most professional paper in Mexico, if not in all of Latin America. Its ideological and editorial slant was progressive and leftist, which in the early-1970s actually coincided with the overall policies of the Echeverría administration. In the initial years of his presidency, Echeverría was known to be very close to Scherer. But the relationship began to deteriorate in 1975 and 1976 as *Excélsior* reporters began to point out some of the hypocrisies in Echeverría's policies, especially his diplomatic moves such as Mexico's support for the U.N. resolution equating Zionism with racism. Echeverría seems to have finally lost patience with Scherer and either directly or indirectly approved plans to oust him and his followers.

The campaign against *Excélsior* began in early 1976 with ads placed in other media outlets attacking *Excélsior* as unpatriotic. Soon the paper's sources began to disappear. The government substantially increased the pressure in June when some 300 peasants and slum dwellers, transported in state-owned buses and headed by a PRI leader from the agrarian sector, "invaded" a parcel of land (218 acres) in the suburbs of Mexico City owned by *Excélsior*. The newspaper had clear title to the land and was legally protected from such invasions. In most cases, the army quickly ousts the invaders. But in this instance government agents helped the squatters with food and even building materials; and *Excélsior* was rebuked in its legal attempts to settle the issue. Finally, the attorney general said that the law could be enforced only after a general assembly of the *Excélsior* cooperative was convened to discuss the issue.

The government had enlisted a group of workers at *Excélsior* (primarily printers) to oppose Scherer. An assembly of the cooperative was held on July 8, which was to be the culmination of the six-month campaign against *Excélsior*. The dissident labor minority, assisted by unidentified, armed men, staged what has been labeled a coup against Scherer and his associates.[19] The Scherer team was shouted down at the meeting, voted out of office by a chaotic voice vote, and forced to vacate its offices. The following day *Excélsior* appeared as a completely sanitized paper under new management (and less some 200 staffers who left with Scherer).

The fallout from the Scherer ouster continued to be felt as late as 1984. Scherer himself successfully started an even more critical publication, the magazine *Proceso*, in November of 1976. *Proceso* has become probably the most important and most aggressive voice for the left in Mexico. Many of the Scherer loyalists also landed on the staff of *Unomásuno*, which became the leading leftist daily in Mexico City. In 1984 some of these same journalists left *Unomásuno* because they felt it had become too close to the government of de la Madrid. They soon established Mexico City's eighteenth daily paper, *La Jornada*, which became the latest print representative for the independent left.

Excélsior received another blow in the murder of its syndicated columnist Manuel Buendía in May of 1984. Buendía had joined *Excélsior* in 1978 to continue writing his popular, daily column "Private Network." Buendía's presence helped restore some of *Excélsior*'s reputation as a critical and independent paper, since he was without a doubt the country's leading investigative reporter (comparisons to columnist Jack Anderson in the United States are frequently made). He was widely regarded as a rare breed of journalist who could not be corrupted, and he had an international following through the syndication of his column in 52 Latin American newspapers.

The targets in Buendía's muckraking column were many and powerful. Corruption among high government officials was one of his favorite issues, and the victims of his attacks on graft included former president López Portillo and two indicted officials, Mexico City Police Chief Arturo Durazo and PEMEX director Jorge Díaz Serrano. Shortly before his death he had also written of corruption in the powerful petroleum workers union. In addition to public corruption, he had been critical of the hierarchy of the Catholic Church in Mexico, leaders of big business, the U.S. government, and ultrarightist groups in Mexico. The last two subjects were even the focus of two of his published books. Buendía was a strong nationalist and even stronger critic of U.S. foreign policies. Two specific antagonists of his writings were the CIA and the U.S. ambassador to Mexico from 1981 until 1986, John Gavin. As a means of chastizing the CIA, he frequently printed the names of individuals he said were CIA agents in Mexico, and one of his books, *The CIA in Mexico*, summarized his criticisms of "The Agency." He specifically criticized Gavin for spending too much time outside of Mexico. Another Buendía book on the threat of ultrarightists in Mexico was published posthumously. In the book he linked former Nicaraguan national guardsmen to the militant ultraright student group, called *Los Tecos*, which is based at the University of Guadalajara. In what may have been an ominous prediction, he had once claimed that they had threatened his life.[20]

Buendía was killed on a crowded street in downtown Mexico City as he was leaving his office near the fashionable Zona Rosa (Pink Zone). He was shot by a single gunman who fired point-blank into his back and escaped on foot down a side street. Buendía clearly was the victim of a professional or contract murder, but the identity of his assailant and the persons behind the killing may never be known. The district attorney first indicated that a political motive had been eliminated as a possibility, but few in Mexico City believed this claim. Most speculation focused on *Los Tecos*, about whom Buendía had most recently written and claimed had threatened him. Other guesses ranged from the CIA to the oil workers union. Regardless of who was responsible, the murder of Buendía was certain to have a chilling effect on independent journalism in Mexico.

In sum, one can see that the Mexican state clearly has enormous powers to stifle freedom of the press. Its mechanisms for control include substantial financial leverage, direct state ownership, guaranteed broadcasting time, harassment, violence, and legal means. The basic press law, passed in 1916, bans "malicious expressions calculated to excite hatred of the authorities, the army, the national guard, or the fundamental institutions of the country."[21] Besides revoking licenses or denying financial subsidies, ultimately the state can expropriate any private-sector holding in the media.

However, despite the potential for state control over the media in Mexico, the government has allowed surprisingly significant freedom of the press, especially for a Latin American nation that is generally labeled authoritarian. While there are many examples of constraints on the print and broadcast media, there are also many cases of unrestrained freedom to criticize the regime or to report events from an independent viewpoint. On balance, and again from the perspective of regional attitudes toward press freedoms, the liberties allowed the media in Mexico probably outweigh the limitations. One analytical survey of freedom of the press in twenty Latin American nations between 1970 and 1975 ranked Mexico among the top four countries in terms of guaranteeing press freedom.[22] Thus, Mexico was placed in the same category as such democracies as Venezuela and Costa Rica.

A multitude of newspapers, magazines, broadcast stations, and publishers exist in Mexico, and they cover the full range of the political spectrum, from leftist publications like *Unomásuno, La Jornada, El Día,* and *Proceso* to rightist papers and magazines such as *El Heraldo, Impacto,* and *Tiempo.* Probably the greatest freedom is enjoyed by the intellectual community and their outlets of expression in scholarly journals and published books. Several centers of higher education in Mexico City (especially UNAM, El Colegio de México, and Centro de Investigación y Docencia Economicas) are bastions of leftist criticism of the capitalist state in Mexico. And these critics are seldom silenced, as they write books, publish in journals and magazines, participate in seminars, and the like.

One illustrative instance occurred in late 1984 when one of Mexico's most noted intellectuals, Pablo González Casanova, received the nation's National Prize for History, Social Sciences, and Philosophy from President de la Madrid. Undoubtedly, the assembled influentials expected González Casanova to offer a gracious acknowledgment for the recognition they were bestowing upon the intellectual community. However, the former rector of UNAM delivered a scathing criticism of the lack of democracy in Mexico.

Of course, one can argue that the intellectual outlets of expression reach a very limited audience. Yet the scholars and commentators still provide a relatively independent and frequently critical source of information available to all citizens. The more sensationalist books, some of which have even begun to criticize the incumbent president (such as López Portillo in his last year in office), have often become best sellers.

The weekly magazines begin to bridge the gap into the more "popular" media. With the exception of *¿Por Qué?,* which openly supported the guerrillas in Guerrero, magazines and weeklies have generally flourished. Scherer's *Proceso* is the single best example of press freedom in Mexico. It has published some of the most vitriolic criticisms of the centers of power in Mexico, without sacrificing its professionalism. Yet it continues to exist, if not prosper, with a national and international readership. At times *Proceso* even violates some of the unwritten rules of Mexican journalism. For example, in the last year of the López Portillo administration, it published a critical exposé of the three luxurious homes the president was having built, allegedly at government expense, on the so-called Hill of the Dogs (a sarcastic commentary on López Portillo's promise to defend the Mexican peso "like a dog" shortly before it was sharply devalued). Another well-known symbol of the political independence of Mexican print media is the political satire of the socialist cartoonist Rius (Eduardo del Río), who irreverently chided such institutions as the PRI, the Catholic Church, the government, and others through his comic books, *Los Supermachos* and *Los Agachados*. Given the enormous popularity of comic books in Mexico, Rius may have had a greater political impact than any other individual in the Mexican media.

The greatest restrictions are reserved for newspapers and the broadcast media, which have the largest audiences. But even here there exist a number of very credible, alternative points of view. As previously mentioned, dozens of daily newspapers exist in Mexico City, representing a full spectrum of editorial opinions. And on the left, where the Mexican state is most sensitive, independent voices like Scherer's *Excélsior* and Buendía's "Private Network" did exist for years; and today the left is well represented by *Unomásuno* and *La Jornada*. Even the generally bland broadcast media provide a few sources of critical expression. The most familiar case is the radio call-in show, *Voz Pública*, hosted weekday mornings by Francisco Huerta with an estimated audience of 1.5 million in Mexico City. Huerta daily listens to citizens' complaints ranging from poor city services to government corruption. In January 1982 López Portillo revoked Huerta's license, but within ten months he had returned to the airwaves uncensored. In the final analysis, the Mexican media enjoy significant freedom and are one of the most important counterweights to state and Party dominance in the Mexican system.

THE PRIVATE SECTOR

Of the groups and institutions outside the PRI, the most powerful and the most independent is the private sector.[23] Only small businesses and some individual entrepreneurs officially belong to the PRI, while the bulk of the Mexican private sector and its political associations remain outside the confines of the Party. The business organizations are in an advantageous position outside the PRI, since they can achieve their objectives through other channels (particularly their trade associations) while escaping the rigors of party discipline.

Though entrepreneurs are not subject to the political controls placed upon the three functional sectors of the Party, the chambers and confederations of industry and commerce are governed by the so-called Chambers Law, which at least provides the potential for strong state control over the private sector. This legislation, which was initiated in 1908 and substantially modified in 1936 and 1941, grants semiofficial status to the chambers, imposes obligatory membership of firms in their sectoral chambers, and allows the state to intervene in various facets of the chambers' operations.

The first Chambers Law (1908) recognized chambers of commerce and industry as "legal personalities" and enumerated their functions. However, the chambers remained largely private and voluntary organizations with significant legal autonomy until the 1936 Chambers Law was passed. As other sectors were being incorporated into the PRI in the 1930s, a new role was being outlined for the industrial and commercial chambers. For the first time, the 1936 law introduced the requirement of obligatory membership for all private firms except the very smallest. The chambers were no longer voluntary organizations, and the 1936 legislation even empowered the state to determine which chamber a firm would join. Chambers were also recognized by the state as "public institutions with juridical personality" and were designated as the representatives of the private sector before the state. In sum, the state was given extensive regulatory powers over the chambers. These legal provisions appeared to give the state considerable leverage in controlling all private-sector chambers and confederations. The state could selectively grant recognition to chambers that were supportive of state policies, and it could force firms to join these semiofficial organizations. The state also had considerable influence over the functions and actions of the chambers through its power to approve many organizational aspects of the chambers.

The actual degree of government control over entrepreneurial groups has not been as great as these legal provisions suggest, however. These powers have seldom if ever been used to intimidate trade associations. Officials from various business chambers and confederations all stated in interviews that their semiofficial status under the Chambers Law was not a hindrance or a constraint.[24] They did not feel that the government controlled their activities, limited their influence, or interfered in their functions. They did state that their guaranteed representation on many state agencies, commissions, and boards along with the requirement that the state must consult with them were definite benefits of their legal status. Many also said that obligatory membership was a positive factor in that it contributed to the unity of the private sector and guaranteed the representation of smaller firms, which otherwise might be apathetic.

Most of the arguments that private-sector organizations are dominated by the state focus on the National Chamber of Manufacturing Industries (Cámara Nacional de la Industria de Transformación, or CANACINTRA). The other two major business groups are the Confederation of National Chambers of Commerce (Confederación de Cámaras Nacionales de Comercio, or CONCANACO) and the Confederation of Industrial Chambers (Confederación de Cámaras Industriales, or CONCAMIN)—both of which are recognized as relatively independent of the state and even as countervailing forces to encroaching government intervention in the economy. But CANACINTRA has been charged as being a "captive group" of the state since its creation in 1941.[25]

Though CANACINTRA is just one of 62 industrial chambers, its size and importance rank it alongside the national confederations. It includes some 60,000 member-firms with most of its members coming from the chemical, automotive, metallurgical, and foodstuffs industries. It is legally a member of CONCAMIN, but it has chosen to operate separately from the industrial confederation.

CANACINTRA was formed less than three months after the new Chambers Law was promulgated. Much of the controversy involving the establishment of CANACINTRA was due to opposition from the commercial chambers, dominant in the private sector until that time, to the 1941 Chambers Law and the 1941 Law of Manufacturing Industries. Commerce and its national confederation, CONCANACO, resented the new emphasis on industrialization and thus worked against not only the 1941 industrial legislation but also the establishment of CANACINTRA, which became a symbol of the industrial revolution in Mexico and of the substantial state role in promoting that revolution.

In reality, CANACINTRA was simply the representative of those new industries that were at the forefront of the state-supported plan of industrialization. Though CANACINTRA opposed the 1942 Trade Agreement with the United States, it favored and benefited from most state policies of the 1940s. This mutually accommodating relationship between the state and CANACINTRA in its early years constitutes the full extent to which the chamber was a "captive group" of the state. CONCAMIN also benefited from the new policies, and its behavior was not terribly different from that of CANACINTRA. Indeed, CANACINTRA's first president (José Cruz y Celis, 1941 to 1943) also served as president of CONCAMIN from 1941 to 1946. In the 1950s even the interests of CONCANACO began to converge more with those of the industrial groups.

The government's coercion of unwilling firms to join or stay in CANACINTRA is mentioned as additional evidence of government control of CANACINTRA. The example most often cited is that of the chemical industry, one of the larger sections of CANACINTRA. Beginning in the late-1950s, certain chemical firms began to petition to leave CANACINTRA and form a separate chamber. The government never permitted the creation of a separate chamber for the chemical industry, but in

1960 a number of chemical industrialists founded the National Chemical Industry Association (Asociación Nacional de Industrias Químicas, or ANIQ), a private, voluntary organization not bound by the Chambers Law. Since then, ANIQ has performed all the functions of a separate chamber and has been affiliated with CONCAMIN. Other large firms have successfully broken with CANACINTRA to form their own chambers to better represent them, such as the National Chamber of the Beer and Malt Industries and the National Chamber of the Perfume and Cosmetic Industries. In addition, regional chambers of manufacturing industries have come into existence, an example being the Chamber of Manufacturing Industries of Nuevo León, established in 1944 as an alternative to CANACINTRA in that northern state.

The ideology of CANACINTRA has suggested to some that it is unrepresentative of the industrial sector and obviously a pawn of the state.[26] Until the 1970s, CANACINTRA professed a very nationalistic doctrine, support for a strong state role in the economy, and a cooperative attitude toward labor. However, these positions were not forced upon the leadership of CANACINTRA by the government; rather, CANACINTRA's philosophy represented the self-interest of its members, which were wholly national-owned, smaller, and newer firms than the commercial firms or the traditional industrial establishments. And as the membership of CANACINTRA has grown and matured, the chamber has adapted its policies to reflect these changes and has become less supportive of government incursions into the economic sphere.[27]

Another argument has been that CANACINTRA is easily manipulated by the state because its presidents always are given important government and Party posts after their presidential terms expire. CANACINTRA's leadership has been viewed as an "unofficial adjunct" of the PRI.[28] However, no firm evidence for this link between CANACINTRA and the state has ever been cited. In fact, no former president of CANACINTRA has ever served in a high government or Party post.

A number of significant private trade associations have been even more autonomous of the state and the PRI than have been CANACINTRA, CONCAMIN, and CONCANACO. Several business sectors (including bankers, insurance firms, foreign trade merchants, and others) have organized as "associations" rather than semiofficial chambers or confederations. These private associations are purely voluntary and do not have to answer to the requirements of the Chambers Law. Though the private associations are more removed from public attention and do not always have the same advantages of representation in state agencies as chambers and confederations, they have played important and often powerful political roles for their members. The associations are not under the guidelines of the Chambers Law, but they can join either the national confederation of commerce or the national confederation of industry and can avail themselves of the confederation's access to the state while retaining their independence from any state control. The major national associations have established their own contacts with the government and at times have aligned with the confederations to form a united front for the private sector before the government.

Another important and independent entrepreneurial group is the Mexican Employers Confederation (Confederación Patronal de la República de México, or COPARMEX). Though COPARMEX is really an employers syndicate under the provisions of the 1931 Labor Law, it has remained a private, voluntary, and fiercely autonomous body. It was established by the influential business leaders of Monterrey and has traditionally been associated with their zealous commitment to free enterprise and limited state intervention in the economy. Even without COPARMEX, the so-called Monterrey Group (some 200 entrepreneurial families whose enterprises contribute almost one-fourth of the nation's total industrial production) is one of the most influential and independent forces in the country. The Monterrey industries, which began with a brewery and a steel mill established before the turn of the century, prospered on their own before the government assumed the role of promoting and protecting manufacturing firms. Thus, the Monterrey Group has never been dependent upon government aid and has always opposed "excessive" government intervention in the economy.

Two final business groups that are both powerful and autonomous are the Mexican Council of Businessmen (Consejo Mexicano de Hombres de Negocios, or CMHN) and the Entrepreneurial Coordinating Council (Consejo Coordinador Empresarial, or CCE). Legally independent from the state, the CMHN is composed of 30 of the most influential businessmen in the country.[29] In addition to being small, it prefers to remain out of the public eye. But, much like the Business Roundtable in the United States, the cohesive and very private CMHN works effectively behind the scenes to influence political decisions crucial to the interests of its powerful members. The CCE was established in 1975 as the umbrella organization for the private sector. It includes representatives of the six major associations and confederations: CONCANACO, CONCAMIN, COPARMEX, CMHN, and the associations for bankers and insurance firms (ABM and AMIS, respectively). Its formation in the last years of the Echeverría administration was a climactic event for the private sector, signifying the desires of business to remain a free and powerful element in Mexican society and to protect the interests of private capital.

Though in many cases the state and the private sector have formed a mutual alliance to promote common interests, business groups have always maintained their autonomy from either government or Party control. This independence was never more obvious than in the aftermath of the bank nationalizations. The decision to nationalize the remaining private banks, which was announced September 1, 1982, in López Portillo's last *Informe*, began a period of discord between the state and the private sector that spilled over into de la Madrid's administration. Soon after the state takeover of the banks, entrepreneurial leaders began to decry what they felt was encroaching "statism" and "socialism." The private sector utilized court cases, public statements, threats of a business strike, and other means of public lobbying in attempts to overturn the decision or dampen its impact. In December of 1982, de la Madrid decided to allow one-third of the banks' stock to be sold to the public.

In addition to protesting the bank decision, private-sector leaders also manifested their opinion that the current political system, as dominated by the PRI, was bent on depriving individuals of their political and economic rights. Once de la Madrid was inaugurated, the private sector focused its attacks on the previous government and the ruling party and was careful not to criticize the new president or his economic team. The split between the private sector and the PRI escalated in January of 1983, when CONCANACO organized a conference in Toluca (with representatives from COPARMEX and the CCE also attending) to criticize the "arbitrary acts" (referring to the bank nationalizations and the exchange controls) of the previous administration. On January 28 the PRI took the unusual step of publishing an advertisement in the major newspapers that was a direct response to the private-sector criticisms. The official party stated that private-sector chambers "are not political institutions nor adequate channels for the expression of ideological positions" and reminded them, in an indirect threat, that they were subject to the control of the Secretary of Commerce and Industrial Promotion. However, indicative of their relative autonomy, the entrepreneurial groups were not intimidated and continued their criticisms of the PRI and the previous government.

Throughout this conflict with the government party, the private-sector leaders clearly differentiated between the PRI and the government of de la Madrid and actually praised the latter. De la Madrid had been the favorite precandidate of business even before his selection by López Portillo; and once de la Madrid was in office, entrepreneurial groups complimented the de la Madrid economic team for taking the "only options available to Mexico" in order to surpass the economic crisis, which the entrepreneurial groups blamed on previous administrations and on a political system dominated by the PRI.

CONCLUSION

In fulfilling its functions of interest mobilization (generating support), education (socialization through propaganda), and conflict resolution (contesting and winning elections), the PRI has attempted to incorporate most of the relevant interest groups into its hierarchical structure. Specifically, the three functional sectors of the Party (labor, agrarian, and popular) represent a significant, if not overwhelming, proportion of organized interests in Mexico, and control over these organs is exercised by the Party president and the National Executive Committee. However, not all political and economic sectors are included within the PRI, and not all groups are effectively controlled or co-opted by the state. Table 9 characterizes the six groups or institutions discussed in this chapter and the previous one, in terms of two dimensions: (1) whether it officially exists within the organizational structure of the PRI or remains outside the framework of the Party; and (2) the degree to which it has been either controlled or co-opted by the state into almost automatic compliance with government dictates. Of the resulting sixfold typology, almost every cell is represented, ranging from the labor and agrarian sectors that have been incorporated into the Party and also readily manipulated by the state to the private sector, which is not only outside the Party but also relatively independent of state control.

The agrarian sector of the PRI (essentially the peasant class) has been the most dependent and least influential of all interest groups. Peasants remain virtually at the mercy of the state, which has retained ultimate authority over the disposition of land. Any militant opposition from the rural sector has been violently repressed by the army. The PRI's labor sector is slightly less subordinate to the state, due to its somewhat greater economic weight. However, the difference between the agrarian and labor sectors in terms of autonomy is minor, and labor

Table 9 Summary of Party and State Dominance of
Six Political Institutions

		Status Vis-à-vis the PRI	
		Within	Outside
Effective Control and/or Co-optation by the State	Yes	Labor Agrarian (peasants)	Military
			Media
	Somewhat	Popular (middle-class)	
	No		Private Sector

has an extremely limited ability to influence policy or to act independently. Even before its official incorporation into the PRM in 1938, organized labor was controlled and co-opted by a mixture of strategies including divide and rule, personal and collective incentives, legal and extralegal repression, and corruption. The third sector within the PRI—the popular sector with middle-class elements such as government employees—has become much more independent of the state. No legal code binds the popular sector to the state, and government workers in particular have established a relationship of reciprocal dependence (or interdependence) with the state. They are provided with jobs and generous benefits, while they in turn provide the state with necessary skills. Their relatively high levels of education and political sophistication have also contributed to their political influence.

The three political forces outside the PRI that have been discussed here are the military, the media, and the private sector. Though they are no longer under the auspices of the Party, the armed services in Mexico have been depoliticized and brought under civilian control. Thus, the military joins the labor and agrarian sectors as being entirely subordinate to the state. These sources of potential instability (revolution from below in the case of labor and peasants, or revolution from above in the case of the military) have been effectively neutralized. The other two societal segments (the media and business), however, have achieved a notable degree of autonomous political power, which has further contributed to the stability of the system as well as preserving some measure of freedom.

The Mexican press and broadcast industries have been granted surprising liberties, and in some cases the media have been highly critical of the state, the Party, or other perceived sources of authoritarian control or economic injustice. Of course, the media's freedom to criticize has served the purposes of the dominant coalition. Critical commentary from the political right actually enhances the revolutionary legitimacy of the state, and the independent leftist media are an important safety valve for intellectuals and dissidents who might otherwise pursue more genuinely revolutionary alternatives. So, the regime calculates the benefits of a free press as outweighing the costs; and whenever the media do pose a threat (for example, *¿Por Qué?* in 1974 or *Excélsior* in 1976), the state will resort to the available mechanisms of control.

The Mexican private sector enjoys an even greater degree of autonomy from the state than do the media. And whereas the media are granted certain freedoms because the regime believes its interests are served best by allowing a relatively free press, the independence of the private sector is more a function of the political and economic power of business. As is the case with the media, the state certainly has the legal capacity for direct intervention in the chambers and confederations of industry and commerce. And the state as an economic actor (in terms of direct state ownership) is significantly more powerful than the private sector. The critical question is why the state has seldom exercised its option to dominate private business. One plausible argument is that the state feels no need to control the business groups because the state and the private sector have a mutual interest in maintaining a capitalist development strategy in Mexico. Thus, neither threatens the other, for they have a common stake in the "alliance for profits." Certainly there is some truth to this argument. However, it ignores an important and inherent degree of independence on the part of the Mexican private sector. For example, when Mexican entrepreneurs felt their basic interests threatened at times by Echeverría, they responded not only with political opposition but with autonomous economic decisions that crippled the economy and contributed to a near political crisis in late 1976 (loss of confidence and rumors of a military coup). The private sector withheld investment during the Echeverría *sexenio*, and in 1976 capital flight from Mexico to the United States reached epidemic proportions.

These actions of the private sector in 1976 showed that the balance of power was not tipped in the direction of the state, that Mexican entrepreneurs wielded considerable economic power that could by used as a political tool, and that the government needed to restore the confidence of Mexican business. López Portillo in his first years established a more harmonious relationship with industry and commerce, but entrepreneurial groups did not sacrifice their independence for more beneficial policies and again stridently criticized government economic policies in 1982.

In general, the private sector has benefited from the national development strategy enacted by the Party in the postwar period, and business is not as strong an electoral opposition group to the Party as is the urban middle class. However, the economic elites are clearly differentiated from and have assumed an adversary relationship with the political elites exemplified by the Party leadership. Many Mexican entrepreneurs belong to opposition parties, particularly the PAN. Previous research has established that the entrepreneurial sector is frequently critical of government economic policies, that the political and economic elites maintain considerable "social distance" from one another, and that the private sector and the PRI are in some cases competing elites.[30] Thus, at least one powerful economic and political actor is not only independent of Party control but also a potential adversary to the Party in the political arena.

7

The PRI and Mexican
Political Elites

The acts of government are not separated from the acts of the party.
—PAN leader and former deputy,
Gonzalo Altamirano Dimas

Previous chapters have examined how major interest groups are linked to the PRI and how opposition parties are allowed to participate in the electoral arena. Such macrolevel analysis is vital to understanding how the PRI has contributed to the stability and legitimacy of the system by incorporating those groups with the greatest revolutionary potential and by permitting the existence (but minimizing the threat) of minority parties. Albeit with some caveats, the PRI has been successful in its dealings with the aggregate political entities (other parties and interest associations). Yet Mexican politics is a very personalistic game, and many of the most relevant relationships are established at an individual level. Thus, the PRI's relationships with individual decision-makers within the political system will be explored.

Given the importance of the Party in providing social services, the blurring of the lines between Party and state at public events, and the overwhelming success of the PRI in the electoral arena, the opening statement of the *panista* Altamirano Dimas, implying that the official party and the government are essentially the same institution, might appear to be an accurate assessment. Are the Party and the state one and the same? Are the personnel in leadership posts in both entities identical? Does one control the other? The answers to these questions will contribute immensely to clarifying the role of the official party in the overall political framework.

THE PARTY AND POLITICAL ELITES

The Local and Elective Level

In examining the connections between the PRI and political elites (the government decision-makers) in Mexico, we need to distinguish between two levels: (1) the local and elective level, and (2) the national and administrative level. At neither level does a perfect unity or total commonality exist between the Party and the government. The ruling party is not the state, and the state is not the ruling party. However, in focusing on the first level in the analysis (local political elites and elective posts), we see that the collaboration between the PRI and the decision-makers is quite close. In fact, there is considerable duplication or overlap of personnel between the Party and local elective positions.

The best evidence available of linkages between the PRI and local government is Susan Eckstein's study of two low-income areas—one a legalized squatter settlement that began with a land invasion and the other a state-constructed housing development in the Federal District.[1] In both locales she found not only a great deal of cooperation between the PRI and government functionaries but considerable shared leadership as well. For example, the two institutions coalesced on many mutually beneficial activites, such as staging public demonstrations and providing health and educational services. Also, PRI officials and local government representatives frequently had daily contact and established close personal bonds. These relationships often produced a "revolving door" between the Party and the state. In some cases, individuals were recruited into government positions because of their Party ties; in other instances, Party leaders were so selected due to their government experience. These various findings led Eckstein to conclude that "in general, there is little difference between the government and the PRI" at the local level.[2]

Another example of Party-state connections, especially at the local and elective level, is the co-called *camarilla*—a network of patron-client relationships that is a very important fact of life in Mexican politics. *Camarillas* are political teams or cliques in which the members are loyal to a single leader who is able to grant political patronage or spoils to his followers. Almost all mobility in the Mexican political system occurs through the *camarillas*. These teams are quite numerous and very competitive, but the Party is the initiating institution for almost all the *camarillas*. The leaders of the *camarillas* (who, in some ways, are the present-day equivalents to the earlier *caudillos*) bring their followers with them as they move into higher and more influential levels of the political system. And the political advancement of a young Party loyalist may be slowed substantially if his patron falls from power.

Roderic A. Camp describes the *camarilla* structure as being pyramidal, with each lower-level pyramid being subsumed by a higher-level one.[3] The overall system, or the primary *camarilla*, is headed by the president of the Republic. Cabinet ministers, top Party leaders, and some heads of major semiautonomous agencies typically head the secondary *camarillas*. The tertiary *camarillas* are led by the top subordinate from the secondary level, and so on. Camp identifies a total of five levels in his analysis of political leaders from 1935 to 1975. Thus, these patron-client ties eventually reach down to the local level, where most political careers begin. Several studies of political career advancements conclude that the first and most necessary step in moving up the political ladder is to join the PRI, followed by working diligently in grassroots Party affairs, and eventually joining a promising *camarilla*.[4]

The reward for the most loyal and diligent Party members is often a seat in the national congress. And most commonly the PRI's candidates are Party functionaries, leaders in affiliated organizations, or local elected officials who previously had served in Party posts. Once elected, many of these individuals stay in their capacity at the PRI (or move to a higher Party job). Table 10 shows the number of federal deputies and senators that filled a coexistent Party post in 1984. The greatest concentration of elected officials was at the highest level within the PRI—the CEN—which had 64 percent of its top positions occupied by members of the congress. The CNOP had 47 percent of its leadership jobs filled by deputies or senators, the CNC had 43 percent, and the CTM had 32 percent. Even within each body, the elected officeholders were disproportionately found at the top of the leadership hierarchy.

An examination of the sectoral loyalties of the PRI delegation in the Chamber of Deputies across time shows how important the popular sector has become since its inception in 1938.[5] The popular sector has consistently provided a majority of the PRI's representation in the lower house (with the exceptions of 1949 and 1976). Thus, if one has ambitions for a congressional seat, the most assured path is to rise through the ranks of the PRI, preferably within the powerful popular sector.

In sum, equating the PRI and the state is a valid conclusion at the local level and in terms of elective posts (short of the presidency of the Republic). PRI district offices are closely intertwined with municipal government officials, the PRI is instrumental in establishing the *camarillas* that begin at the local level, and the Party is the major source or channel for upward mobility into the national congress (where the federal deputies and senators frequently retain their Party leadership positions).

Table 10 Federal Deputies and Senators in Party Leadership Positions, 1984

Party Organ	Total No. of Top Positions	No. of Top Positions Filled By:		
		Deputies	Senators	Other
CEN	30	11 (37%)	8 (27%)	11[a]
CNOP	28	10 (36%)	3 (11%)	15
CNC	32	11 (34%)	3 (9%)	18
CTM	22	5 (23%)	2 (9%)	15

Source: Partido Revolucionario Institucional, unpublished documents.
[a] Three of these are military men.

The National and Administrative Level

A second tier of political power rests in the national elites (principally the president of Mexico and the federal bureaucracy). Three major points will underline the discussion of Party-state relations at this level. First, the presidency and the federal bureaucracy wield most of the political power in Mexico. Second, this level represents a very distinctive career path with few connections to the local and elective level. And third, the PRI does not play a significant role in the recruitment process for the national and administrative elites.

The Mexican political system is a very centralized structure with political power concentrated in the office of the president. The Mexican state is a federal republic in name only. In reality, it verges on being a unitary system—concentrating authority at the national level. Though separate legislative and judicial branches exist, the president uses his formal and informal powers to dominate the decision-making process. The national congress is little more than a rubber stamp to the executive branch, and the judicial branch seldom demonstrates any independence from the president. The president can almost guarantee the passage of his legislative proposals by the congress, can transfer budgetary funds and even exceed authorized expenditures, and can affect policy through *reglamentos* (a form of clarification issued after the promulgation of a law) and presidential decrees (emergency powers only).

In addition to making all cabinet-level appointments, the president selects the secretary-general and president of the Party and the leaders of the PRI in congress. In fact, probably the most significant source of presidential power is his role as Party chief. At the national level, the PRI as an institution is not on equal footing with the state, especially the president. If anything, the president controls the Party. Besides the aforementioned Party appointments, the president has substantial influence over the selection process for PRI candidates to elected positions above the local level.

The cabinet-level posts also wield considerable influence. They are accountable only to the president, are often given substantial discretionary powers, and in many cases are directly involved in the policy-making process.[6] Traditionally considered the most influential cabinet position is the secretary of *gobernación*, which is responsible for internal security and also oversees the electoral process. The secretary of finance, together with the head of the central bank (Banco de México), exercises significant influence over fiscal and monetary policies. The secretary of commerce and industrial promotion focuses on other issues of importance to business, from international trade to domestic prices. Finally, the secretary of programming and budget has the tasks of formulating the budget and devising economic plans. These four ministries are generally recognized as the "inner" cabinet—the most influential advisers with the closest contact to the president. However, other cabinet posts such as labor, foreign relations, education, and agrarian reform frequently assume a great deal of power. All together, the president and his cabinet are essentially the power structure in Mexican politics and dominate all other governmental institutions as well as the Party.

A superficial argument could be made that the president, as the PRI candidate, is somewhat beholden to the Party for nominating and electing him to the highest office in the country. However, this argument ignores the reality of the presidential selection process in Mexico, in which the incumbent, lame-duck president unilaterally handpicks his successor. Though scholars have not yet uncovered all the machinations of the highly secretive process, the autonomous power of one president to select the next president is indisputable. And possibly as a deliberate means of emphasizing this choice as solely a presidential prerogative, the process has remained essentially "arbitrary and capricious."[7] As one example, in 1976 when Echeverría purposely did not pick the favored and expected candidate, Mario Moya Palencia (the secretary of *gobernación*), and instead "tapped" his finance minister, López Portillo, as his heir to the presidential sash. This surprising move reintroduced the concept of uncertainty in the process, thereby reifying the image of the president's authority to choose his successor independently of traditional norms or popular favorites. In any case, the president is not indebted to the Party for his selection but only to his predecessor, who by another unwritten rule of Mexican politics should fade quickly from the public eye.

The subordination of the Party to the president (even to the presidential nominee) was quite evident in the presidential transitions of 1975–1976 and 1981–1982. The president of the PRI in 1975, Jesús Reyes Heroles, planned to formulate a party platform prior to the designation of the presidential candidate. But Echeverría humiliated both Reyes Heroles and the Party by naming López Portillo before the platform was completed. López Portillo quickly took control of the preparations for the platform and the general campaign, and Reyes Heroles was demoted to the social security institute.

Almost the same circumstances repeated themselves in the transition to de la Madrid. Only days after de la Madrid was "tapped" by López Portillo in September 1981, Carlos Salinas de Gortari became head of the Institute for Political, Economic, and Social Studies of the PRI, and in this capacity he quickly presented a *Plan Básico* (actually the party platform) to the National Assembly of the PRI on October 5.[8] This marked the beginning of "democratic planning" under the president-to-be, though it really was the continuation of a planning team that was first formed when de la Madrid became minister of planning and budget in May 1979 and Salinas de Gortari directed the studies for the *Plan Global de Desarrollo* (a very broad national development plan) within the same ministry. However, the Party as an independent actor had negligible input into the formulation of the platform. In fact, Party efforts to draft a platform prior to October 1981 were scrapped by Salinas de Gortari, who quickly put together a document representing the political priorities and philosophy of de la Madrid. Though Salinas de Gortari was at that time in a Party post, his loyalties were to de la Madrid and not to the Party establishment (which, as we shall see, were not equivalent).

This *Plan Básico*, which de la Madrid and Salinas de Gortari had created as the PRI's platform, was the basis from which the *Plan Nacional de Desarrollo, 1983–1988* (later publicized as the blueprint for the de la Madrid *sexenio*) evolved. But the process leading from the party platform to the national development plan was slow and arduous. The PRI was involved in the planning framework, but its role was simply that of a mouthpiece for the de la Madrid team. In October 1981 de la Madrid announced that the *Plan Básico* would be analyzed by the PRI in consultation with the Mexican people. During the next eight months of the election campaign, over 100 public meetings were held under this "popular consultation" with all social, political, and economic sectors. On June 2, 1982, Salinas de Gortari summarized the results of these and first presented the basic themes later to be emphasized in de la Madrid's inaugural address. The planning hierarchy was expanded on July 20, when the PRI formed 27 working groups to analyze the information collected over the previous eight months of "popular consultation."

On January 5, 1983, a new Planning Law was promulgated which did little more than institutionalize the "popular consultation" and establish a National System of Democratic Planning.[9] Under this National System, the president installed eighteen forums in early February (covering different economic and social sectors) that would hold more public meetings regarding the formulation of the National Plan. These forums and the creation of the new Plan were coordinated by the new minister of programming and budget, Carlos Salinas de Gortari.[10] As with the multitude of previous meetings, these forums were designed more for public consumption than for legitimate public or even Party input. Almost all of the public forums were announced only a day or two before they took place, and participants were required to submit their statements in advance.

The *Plan Nacional de Desarrollo, 1983–1988* (or PND) was finally announced by de la Madrid on May 30, 1983. It contained no surprises and essentially elaborated the policies and objectives already put forth by the new administration. The economic and social strategy of the PND was summarized in six areas, which were remarkably similar to the themes presented by Salinas de Gortari in June of 1982 and to the recovery program announced by de la Madrid in his inaugural address. Thus, the various Party working groups and the months of popular consultations and public forums had little impact on a national plan that essentially had been devised by de la Madrid and a small group of close advisers in 1981 and 1982.

As mentioned previously, the career path into the national and administrative elite roles is generally independent of the pattern of mobility into the local and elective elite positions.[11] While the most common preparation for mayors, federal deputies, and even senators and governors is loyal service in the Party and its sectoral organizations, the career background of presidents and cabinet heads is becoming increasingly concentrated in the federal bureaucracy itself. Furthermore, there is little movement from the elective posts into the national elite level. The era when the president and ministers had served some time in elective posts is quickly fading into history. One of the most repeated and telling facts about recent trends in Mexican political recruitment is that Echeverría, López Portillo, and de la Madrid never held an elective position prior to the presidency. Federal deputyships, in particular, have become dead-end posts. The probability of using a seat in the federal Chamber as a springboard to higher office is becoming increasingly negligible. Even governors and federal senators do not have a strong chance of moving into the cabinet or subcabinet level. Thus, most national and administrative elites began their political careers at lower rungs of the federal bureaucratic ladder and slowly worked their way to the top.

In addition to spending their entire careers in the bureaucracy, national elites also tend to share three other background traits: residency in the Federal District, growing specialization in graduate fields other than law, and education at the National University (UNAM). The three most recent presidents were either born or raised (or both) in the Federal District, and even the members of recent cabinets tend to be natives of the nation's capital.[12] Regarding fields of academic concentration, national elites in Mexico over the last decade or so are coming increasingly from academic areas besides law, which previously had dominated the educational training of top officials.[13] Though law remains the single largest discipline from which the nation's elite emerges, economics and engineering are rapidly closing the gap. This trend for political elites to have technical training is actually a phenomenon that has become endemic to Latin America. A related tendency in Mexico is to acquire a graduate degree from a foreign university, typically an institution in the United States or Europe. De la Madrid is an excellent and current example of having pursued advanced training abroad, as he received a master's degree in public administration from Harvard University in the mid-1960s.

The final characteristic common to most high-ranking federal officials is time spent at UNAM as students and in many cases as professors as well. The National University has always been internationally respected for its academic achievements. In recent years (possibly due to its academic reputation) it has also become popular for being a prime (almost necessary) breeding ground for national politicians. Established in 1551, UNAM is one of the oldest academic institutions in the region, has become one of the largest universities in the world, and as its formal name—the National Autonomous University of Mexico—implies, has retained its independence from outside political pressures.[14] Many student leaders are recruited straight from the campus of UNAM to the offices of the federal bureaucracy, and an astonishingly large number of governing elites are from UNAM. In his analysis of political elites, Peter Smith found that about 70 percent of the postwar "upper elites" came from UNAM and that 65 percent of the cabinet officials had studied at the National University.[15] Many of the top bureaucrats have even taught at UNAM—over half of López Portillo's highest-ranking appointees had done so. A faculty slot almost seems to have become a prerequisite for the presidency, as Presidents Echeverría, López Portillo, and de la Madrid served stints as professors at UNAM.

The national and administrative elites, therefore, tend to be lifelong bureaucrats with no experience in elective politics, graduates of the National University, and increasingly specialists in technical fields such as economics and engineering (frequently receiving such training abroad). In sum, *políticos* (political leaders who have spent most of their careers in and around elective politics and associated with Party sectoral organizations) are rapidly being replaced by *técnicos* (decision-makers who have technical training and have been in the administrative arena throughout their professional lives) in the top ranks of Mexican politics.[16] The Party, particularly the sectoral affiliates, has become much less significant in the recruitment and preparation of national elites. The typical union leader or secretary-general of a party organ, who possesses considerable skills in mass-based political organizing, is now generally irrelevant to the upper echelons of the political elite. The *técnicos*, whose skills are more specialized, are clearly on the ascent.[17] Their strengths are geared more toward problem-solving in the technical areas (i.e., economics, administration, engineering, health, and so on) rather than toward understanding the realities of the political sphere. The advent of these *técnicos* may be the most important phenomenon in Mexican politics today.

CAREER PATHS OF RECENT PRESIDENTS AND CABINET OFFICIALS

An examination of the major career steps of Mexican presidents since Alemán (the first noncivilian) demonstrates several outstanding characteristics of the national political elite (see Table 11). The most obvious, and probably the most significant, fact is that every president came directly from a cabinet-level post, which underlines the political influence of the bureaucracy in Mexico. This pattern is quite different from the United States experience, where presidents tend to have been in other elective positions (usually governor, senator, or vice president) prior to their election as president. Potential Mexican presidents serve their most important apprenticeship in the cabinet, which has substantial policy-making responsibilities in addition to its role in the presidential succession process. One cabinet ministry has been especially salient in producing presidents: the secretary of *gobernación*. Four of the seven presidents since 1946 came from *gobernación* (Alemán, Ruiz Cortines, Díaz Ordaz, and Echeverría).[18] However, a signficant trend may be indicated by the fact that the two most recent presidents (López Portillo and de la Madrid) spent almost all of their careers in the economic or technocratic ministries.

A second characteristic, which was emphasized previously, is the common experience of a degree from the National University. And whereas a growing proportion of nonlaw degrees is noticeable at lower

Table 11   Career Paths of Mexican Presidents Since 1946

Alemán, 1946–1952
Law degree, UNAM
↓
PNR post (minor)[a]
↓
Senator
↓
Governor
↓
Cabinet
↓
President

Ruiz Cortines, 1952–1958
PRI post (minor)[a]
↓
Bureaucracy
↓
Deputy
↓
Subcabinet
↓
Governor
↓
Cabinet
↓
President

López Mateos, 1958–1964
PNR post (minor)[a]
↓
Law degre, UNAM
↓
Bureaucracy
↓
Senator
↓
PRI post (major)[a]
↓
Cabinet
↓
President

Díaz Ordaz, 1964–1970
Law degree, University of
Puebla
↓
Deputy
↓
Senator
↓
Subcabinet
↓
Cabinet
↓
President

Echeverría, 1970–1976
Law degree, UNAM
↓
Law professor, UNAM
↓
PRI post (major)[a]
↓
Bureaucracy
↓
Subcabinet
↓
PRI post (major)[a]
↓
Subcabinet
↓

López Portillo, 1976–1982
Law degree, UNAM
↓
Law professor, UNAM
↓
PRI post (minor)[a]
↓
Bureaucracy
↓
Subcabinet
↓
Cabinet
↓
President

Table 11 Career Paths of Mexican Presidents Since 1946

Cabinet
↓
President

de la Madrid, 1982–1988
Law degree, UNAM
↓
Law professor, UNAM
↓
Bureaucracy
↓
Subcabinet
↓
Cabinet
↓
President

Source: Camp, *Mexican Political Biographies.*
[a] A major Party post is one at the level of the CEN.

levels of the bureaucracy, all presidents have acquired their degrees in law. Even one of the non-UNAM graduates, Díaz Ordaz, had a law degree from the University of Puebla, where he eventually became vice-rector. Ruiz Cortines has the unique distinction of being the only postwar president with no degree, as he had to quit school early in life to support his family. In addition to the UNAM degree, the last three presidents spent some time studying abroad and also served as professors of law at the National University after completing their studies. Echeverría studied in South America, Europe, and the United States; López Portillo earned a second law degree from the University of Santiago, Chile; and de la Madrid acquired a master's degree from Harvard.

The third noteworthy characteristic of presidential career paths is the lack of any strong linkages with the ruling party. Only two of the seven postwar presidents have any background in a major Party position. López Mateos served a brief period as secretary-general of the PRI in 1951 prior to running the presidential campaign of Ruiz Cortines in 1952.[19] Echeverría had the strongest Party connections, having entered politics in 1946 by joining the PRI and the *camarilla* of the Party president at that time. He soon rose to become press secretary for the CEN and remained in that capacity for six years. In 1957 he returned to a top Party job as *Oficial Mayor* of the PRI until 1958, when he became subsecretary of *gobernación*. His early and significant ties to the PRI, however, are clearly the exception. Even López Mateos came to a major Party position only after time in the bureaucracy. All other presidents succeeded to that high office without any major Party responsibilities.

The final point, or really a trend that has been noted above, is the declining importance of elective posts in the backgrounds of Mexican presidents. Through Díaz Ordaz, all postwar Mexican presidents had served previously as a federal deputy, senator, and/or state governor. However, beginning with Echeverría this experience in the electoral arena seems to have become irrelevant. The dearth of any prior electoral background for the three latest presidents is one of the strongest indicators of the dominance of the bureaucracy and the technocrats in Mexican politics.

An overview of the career characteristics of the initial cabinet of de la Madrid (as of December 1982) provides an even stronger indication of the technocratic backgrounds of the national political elite. Table 12 sketches briefly characteristics of each cabinet official: a degree from UNAM, studies abroad, a technocratic degree, no strong Party ties, or no experience in an elective post. As would be expected, UNAM proves to be a major part of the career preparations of most of the cabinet. Of the eleven cabinet members for which such information was available, nine had degrees from UNAM. Furthermore, six had taught at UNAM, and one was even rector (Soberón Acevedo, from 1973 until 1981). Eight of the cabinet heads had taken advanced degrees in universities outside of Mexico, including four technocratic degrees: Salinas de Gortari (Ph.D. in economics from Harvard), Enríquez Savignac (master's in business administration from Harvard), Silva Herzog (master's in economics from Yale), and Hernández Cervantes (master's in economics from the University of Melbourne). All together, ten of the sixteen ministers had technocratic degrees.

In terms of their Party linkages and their involvement in electoral politics, their political backgrounds are quite sparse. Only five had served in a major Party post, and four of these were appointed to their positions by the president of the Republic after illustrious bureaucratic careers. Bartlett Díaz was named secretary-general of the PRI after having served in finance, *gobernación*, foreign relations, and programming (as well as having been secretary-general of the CNC in the early 1960s). As part of his Party responsibilities, he headed the campaign of de la Madrid in 1982. Bernardo Sepúlveda and Salinas de Gortari also spent their only time in the upper echelons of the PRI during the de la Madrid campaign, as secretary of foreign relations and head of the IEPES, respectively. Ojeda Paullada was appointed president of the PRI for a brief period after lengthy subcabinet tenures in PEMEX, the ministries

Table 12 Characteristics of Initial de la Madrid Cabinet

Cabinet Official	A	B	C	D	E
Gobernación					
(Bartlett Díaz)	X	X			X
Finance					
(Silva Herzog)	X	X	X	X	X
Commerce					
(Hernández Cervantes)	X	X	X	X	X
Industry					
(Labastida Ochoa)	n.a.	n.a.	X	X	X
Programming					
(Salinas de Gortari)	n.a.	X	X		X
Labor					
(Farell Cubillas)	X			X	X
Foreign Relations					
(Bernardo Sepúlveda)	X	X			X
Education					
(Reyes Heroles)	X	X			
Agrarian Reform					
(Martínez Villicaña)			X	X	X
Attorney General					
(García Ramírez)	X			X	X
Agriculture					
(García Aguila)			X	X	X
Communications					
(Félix Valdés)	n.a.	n.a.	X	X	X
Public Works					
(Javelly Girard)	n.a.	n.a.		X	X
Health					
(Soberón Acevedo)	X	X	X	X	X
Tourism					
(Enríquez Savignac)	n.a.	X	X	X	X
Fisheries					
(Ojeda Paullada)	X		X		X

Sources: Camp, *Mexican Political Biographies;* and Presidencia de la República, *El Gobierno Mexicano,* no. 1 (Mexico: Dirección General de Comunicación Social, December 1982), pp. 30–36.

Note: An "X" indicates that the characteristic does apply to the cabinet official. An "n.a." denotes that no information was available. In terms of each characteristic:
    A = UNAM degree;
    B = Advanced studies abroad;
    C = Technocratic degree;
    D = No major Party post; and
    E = No elective post.

of health and natural resources, and the secretary of the presidency and after serving in the cabinet as attorney general and secretary of labor.

Reyes Heroles (who died in 1985) was the only true Party veteran in the original de la Madrid cabinet.[20] He began his political career in the PRM in 1939, as auxiliary private secretary for the CEN president, and served in other Party posts until becoming Party president in 1972 (remaining there until being replaced by López Portillo in 1975). Reyes Heroles is also the only cabinet member to have been elected to a public office. From 1961 to 1964 he was the federal deputy from the second district in the powerful state of Veracruz. Thus, the venerable Reyes Heroles was the lone *político* in the initial de la Madrid cabinet, while the remaining secretaries were classic *técnicos*, with few Party ties, lifelong public careers in the bureaucracy, and frequently technical degrees.

THE SUBORDINATION OF THE PRI

This chapter began with a quote implying that the PRI coexists with the state. A discussion of ties between PRI officials and local and elective elites showed that the Party and the government have become closely intertwined at the local level. The two institutions share many overlapping officials, and the PRI has been essential for career advancement in local and elective positions.

However, the Party in many ways is a very fragile institutional actor. In the first place, its membership is very fluid and inconsistent. Since Party membership and participation are not strictly voluntary acts (motivated usually by material incentives), identification with the PRI is not strong ideologically. In times of economic hardship, the Party has to depend upon the decades of socialization and indoctrination to maintain the loyalty of its supporters. Some indications in the early years of the de la Madrid administration suggested that this loyalty may be slipping from the grasp of the Party hierarchy.

Furthermore, the PRI is not significant in the background of the national political elites, where power really resides in the Mexican system. The National University and the federal bureaucracy itself have become more important training grounds and sources of political patronage than the Party. Therefore, a new class of technocrats with very few Party ties is becoming the dominant force in Mexican politics.

Though the bureaucrats are in ascendance, they certainly accept the role of the PRI as a crucial ally in running the country. The Party clearly does not control the reins of political decision-making, nor is it even a coequal to the state. Yet most national elites are at least Party members, and more significantly, the Party is a very critical institution serving the executive branch of government, particularly the office of the presidency. Especially with national elites becoming so technocratic, the PRI provides the president with the necessary political legitimacy, the symbolic aura of the Revolution, and the machinery for running campaigns, winning elections, and maintaining contacts with the masses. The presidential nominee establishes his political mandate during the months of a whirlwind campaign that takes him to every corner of the nation. And during the *sexenio* the president continues a rapid pace of ceremonial visits (called *giras de trabajo*) throughout Mexico to inaugurate governors, tour facilities, cut ribbons, and the like. In both cases, the Party apparatus plays the major role in organizing the events.

The president of the Republic definitely controls the PRI. He appoints the Party president and secretary-general and at least approves the other members of the CEN and all PRI electoral nominees to the national congress. Those cabinet members who served in a Party role, such as Bartlett Díaz, Bernardo Sepúlveda, and Salinas de Gortari in de la Madrid's cabinet, usually were put into those positions by the presidential nominee during the campaign. By appointing his "own men" to these crucial Party posts, the president-to-be is seizing the reins of power in the PRI—often ousting more independent Party veterans in the process (such as Reyes Heroles in 1975). The Party, however, remains an essential pillar of support for the national elites. The president and his cabinet may be dominant, but the PRI is still an indispensable source of political legitimacy.

8

Challenges Facing the PRI and Mexico

He will not finish his six-year term. He has lost control of the country.

—Hector Riva Palacio,
conservative senator whose grandfather was a PRI founder,
on de la Madrid

On the one hand, the PRI has been a major contributor to the successes in Mexican political and economic history: the decades of political stability along with reasonable economic success under a benignly authoritarian government in which political repression is not overt and certain groups are allowed considerable autonomy. On the other hand, the PRI is currently facing its greatest challenges on both the electoral front (setbacks in 1982 and 1983) and the administrative front (the advent of *técnicos*). Some view the challenges so great as to forecast the end of political stability in Mexico.[1]

The longevity of the PRI is indeed remarkable given the lack of any historical predecessors in the nineteenth century. Born in the throes of the region's first mass-based revolution in the present century, the ruling party has amassed a record of almost six decades of political dominance, in which it has never lost a presidential or gubernatorial race and very few congressional, state, or local contests. Yet political stability has been maintained with very little overt political repression. In fact, an aura of democratic legitimacy has been established through the political reform that has allowed up to eight opposition parties to contest presidential and congressional races. Essentially, the Party has contributed to political stability in two ways: the incorporation of most interest groups and the maintenance of a delicate political balance.

The PRI has accomplished the most effective control and co-optation over those groups with the greatest revolutionary or counterrevolutionary potential (labor, peasants, and the military). Even the timing of this incorporation (which was virtually completed in the 1930s) prior to entering the phase of capital accumulation (which began in the 1940s) enabled Mexico to avoid the destabilizing factors that plagued Argentina and Brazil.[2] Those groups with the greatest economic and political power (the middle class, media, private sector, intellectuals, and academic community) have been allowed the greatest freedoms—partially as a safety valve to release political frustrations and partially as a means of insuring political legitimacy. Though some remain unincorporated, all groups have been induced by the regime at various times through rewards and incentives, which have played an important part in establishing a political balance.

This political balance refers to creating a policy equilibrium between the political left and the political right in Mexico. One aspect of this balancing act has already been discussed: the so-called pendulum effect in which successive presidential terms swing from one side of the political spectrum to another. Though empirical analysis proves that the differences between *sexenios* in terms of both the policy output and the policy impact are actually negligible, the political perceptions of differences are quite real.[3] In a political sense, the perceptions of such shifts in the minds of the groups being placated are more significant than the reality. Echeverría was viewed as a populist president who courted labor and other progressive forces while alienating the domestic and foreign private sector. López Portillo (at least until his last year in office) was seen as a friend of business who was committed to the restoration of economic confidence. Though these political moves were initiated in the executive branch, the Party machinery loyally supported and publicized each new presidential program.

A second aspect of this political balance is the coexistence across time of a generally conservative domestic policy with a more leftist foreign policy. Despite the nationalizations and rhetoric of some of the left-leaning presidents, Mexican economic policy has consistently emphasized capital accumulation over redistribution. The postwar development strategies—from import substitution to the oil boom to the present policy of export substitution—have all favored the private sector over labor and peasants. Presidents may complain about the excesses of big business and foreign capital; and strikes and demands for wage increases may dominate the headlines. But the true story is the success of private entrepreneurs, in alliance with the state, in sustaining economic growth along with monetary stability. Even when the economic crisis hit Mexico in 1982, the response was one of the most severe austerity programs in the region, which forced the lower-income groups to shoulder a disproportionate share of the burden. The political right in Mexico clearly has been the dominant voice concerning domestic economic policy, and the private sector has been the major benefactor of postwar development strategies.

The political left, however, has been mollified by a progressive foreign policy, which the PRI has been especially proud to extoll. As the Party of the Revolution, the PRI has emphasized foreign policy as a means of solidifying its revolutionary legitimacy. Mexico has gone beyond the principle of self-determination to support various leftist and revolutionary movements with which it has sympathized. As far back as the 1930s, it sided with the Soviet Union in aiding the Spanish Republic against Franco. In the 1950s and 1960s Mexico was the only Latin American nation not to break diplomatic and commercial relations with Cuba. Echeverría in the 1970s maintained very close and friendly ties with the leftist military government in Peru and the socialist government under Allende in Chile. Most recently, even under the more conservative López Portillo, Mexico publicly supported the Sandinista insurrection against Somoza in Nicaragua.

A number of reasons can be cited for this leftist tilt in foreign policy. One is simply Mexico's revolutionary heritage. Whether sincere or not, Mexican leaders have always adopted sympathetic policies toward other revolutionary movements. To do otherwise would be interpreted as a denial of Mexico's own revolution. This factor has been critical to the PRI's support for Mexico's nonaligned foriegn policy. Another reason is basically geographic. As the nation on the poor side of the longest border in the world between an advanced, industrial state and a developing Third World nation, Mexico feels a necessity to assert its independence from its northern neighbor. Historical experience with U.S. intervention and loss of territory have further heightened the anti-U.S. strain in Mexico's international policies. A final reason for the left-leaning foreign policy relates to the restoration of a political balance in Mexico and to the domestic functions of foreign policy. While the Mexican Revolution may indeed by dead at home, it lives on in Mexico's support for revolutionary causes beyond its borders. A progressive approach to international affairs has been an easy way to counterbalance a conservative domestic policy.[4]

Because of this effort to maintain a political equilibrium between the left and the right, the ideology or doctrine of the PRI is difficult to categorize. It promotes itself as a left-of-center party and identifies with the international Social Democratic movement. But its ideology is really one of political pragmatism. The Party can shift its philosophy in one direction or another and can favor first one group then another—always attempting to preserve the stability of the system and placate any disaffected groups. Ideology becomes another tool to be used in maintaining the regime and the dominant coalition.

Thus, through astute efforts at interest group incorporation and political balancing, the PRI has promoted the stable political base which in turn has been an important factor in the relative economic success of postwar Mexico. But the Party does face some significant threats to both its own position and the regime's stability in the 1980s. The first, and probably most important, challenge to the Party is the growing influence of a new technocratic ruling class.[5] The traditional Party elite, based in the sectoral affiliates, is fast becoming a powerless group. The PRI is controlled by the president of the Republic and his most loyal advisers, who together comprise the national political elite. At least since Echeverría, this political elite has been primarily characterized as technocratic, specialized, and managerial. While these skills may be well suited for attacking the economic difficulties of the 1980s, they may be useless in solving the political problems. For example, the *técnicos* can devise the austerity measures leading to an economic recovery, but they may be incapable of "selling" their program to the public. The traditional political skills of organizing and manipulating the masses may be required to exact the necessary long-term sacrifices from the Mexican people. A plausible argument can be made that the ascent of *técnicos* has left the national elite out of touch with the citizenry and the mass-based organizations.

While bureaucrats with technical backgrounds tend to dominate the highest levels of power, the PRI remains more oriented toward the political and sectoral leaders at the intermediate level of Mexican politics. Above the Party are the independently minded *técnicos*, and below it are the masses who grow increasingly out of touch with both the Party and the administrative elite. With the passing of the old-line political bosses like Velásquez of the CTM, the Party may be able to reform internally and establish closer links with both its rank-and-file membership and the governing *técnicos*. The short-term probabilities, however, are not promising, as evidenced by Party actions in the 1985 elections. Despite promises of fairer elections by national Party leaders (including de la Madrid), traditional activists at the state and local levels apparently resorted to the usual tactics of electoral fraud to insure a landslide PRI victory at the polls. They were not willing to grant the genuine liberalization within and outside the Party needed to enhance the Party's democratic image and strengthen the PRI's popular appeal.

The declining attention given to political skills and the growing gap between the Party and the masses in part have produced the second challenge to the Party: deteriorating support and electoral setbacks. The economic crisis of the 1980s dealt the Party and the governing elite a severe blow. Whereas the PRI previously depended upon economic growth as the basis for insuring its popular support, after the crisis it faced the challenge of adopting policies of democratization and more ideological rigor in order to solidify its identification with the electorate. In 1982 de la Madrid polled the lowest proportion of the total vote ever for a PRI candidate. The Party was beginning to show particular weaknesses among the urban middle class and in the central and northern states. The 1983 state and local elections then produced the worst defeats for the ruling party at those levels. Electoral victories in 1984 were achieved at the cost of widespread charges of fraud and surprising outbreaks of political violence. Recognizing the growing popular disaffection with the ruling party and the importance of the 1985 elections, the PRI met in 1984 for the 55th Anniversary of its founding (in March) and for its Twelfth National Assembly (in August) under the slogan of "reform and renovation." However, the 1985 elections showed no evidence of the reform.

The PRI has weathered crises before and more than likely will survive the present challenges. Indeed, a greater crisis facing Mexico than either the political legitimacy of *técnicos* or the electoral decline of the ruling party is the crisis of presidential succession. The transfer of presidential power every six years has been plagued with problems. Capital flight, devaluations, drastic nationalizations and expropriations, rumors of military coups, and charges of corruption seem increasingly to characterize the final year of a *sexenio*. This instability has been fueled by the inability to seek reelection, the desire to accomplish much before leaving office, public anticipation of a new president a full two years prior to the transfer of power, and the impending massive change in administrative posts. This difficulty of a lame-duck president wanting to leave a historical legacy while the people impatiently await a new leader requires a constitutional solution and is not a direct challenge to the Party. Yet the problems of the Party on both the administrative and the electoral fronts are not negligible and will necessitate innovative changes. While the 1984 slogan of "reform and renovation" produced no concrete results, the rhetoric will have to turn to reality if the PRI is to adapt to a more complex and unpredictable political situation.

Notes

CHAPTER 1

1. *Washington Post*, July 14, 1968.
2. Economic data are from The World Bank, *World Development Report 1983* (New York: Oxford University Press, 1983), pp. 148–67.
3. For data and discussions of this issue, see Roger D. Hansen, *The Politics of Mexican Development* (Baltimore: The John Hopkins University Press, 1974), pp. 71–95; Daniel Levy and Gabriel Székely, *Mexico: Paradoxes of Stability and Change* (Boulder, Colo.: Westview Press, 1983), pp. 141–44; and The World Bank, *World Development Report 1980*, pp. 156–57.
4. Robert E. Scott, *Mexican Government in Transition* (Urbana: University of Illinois Press, 1964), p. 300. Also, John Booth and Mitchell Seligson cite survey research to show that "urban Mexicans of both middle- and working-class status demonstrated strong support for democratic liberties." John A. Booth and Mitchell A. Seligson, "The Political Culture of Authoritarianism in Mexico: A Reexamination," *Latin American Research Review* 19, 1 (1984): 118.
5. Pablo González Casanova, *Democracy in Mexico* (New York: Oxford University Press, 1970), p. 157.
6. U.S. Department of State, "Democracy in Latin America and the Caribbean" (Washington: Bureau of Public Affairs, 1984).
7. Philippe C. Schmitter, "Still the Century of Corporatism?" *The Review of Politics* 36, 1 (January 1974): 96.
8. Ibid., p. 93.
9. See James Cockroft, *El imperialismo, la lucha de clases y el estado en México* (Mexico: Editorial Nuestro Tiempo, 1980); Nora Hamilton, *The Limits of State Autonomy: Post-Revolutionary Mexico* (Princeton, N.J.: Princeton University Press, 1982); and James Cockroft, *Mexico: Class Formation, Capital Accumulation, and the State* (New York: Monthly Review Press, 1983).
10. Juan J. Linz, "An Authoritarian Regime: The Case of Spain," in Erik Allardt and Stein Rokkan, eds., *Mass Politics: Studies in Political Sociology* (New York: Free Press, 1970), pp. 251–83; and Susan Kaufman Purcell, "Decision-Making in an Authoritarian Regime: Theoretical Implications from a Mexican Case Study," *World Politics* 26, 1 (October 1973): 28–54.
11. Another significant contribution by Susan Kaufman Purcell in this area is her book *The Mexican Profit-Sharing Decision: Politics in an Authoritarian Regime* (Berkeley: University of California Press, 1975). See also Evelyn P. Stevens, "Protest Movement in an Authoritarian Regime: The Mexican Case," *Compar-*

ative Politics 7, 3 (April 1975): 361–82; Merilee S. Grindle, "Policy Change in an Authoritarian Regime: Mexico Under Echeverría," *Journal of Interamerican Studies and World Affairs* 19, 4 (November 1977): 523–55; José Luis Reyna and Richard S. Weinert, eds., *Authoritarianism in Mexico* (Philadelphia: Institute for the Study of Human Issues, 1977); and Peter H. Smith, *Labyrinths of Power: Political Recruitment in Twentieth-Century Mexico* (Princeton, N.J.: Princeton University Press, 1979).

12. In discussing specific aspects of authoritarian control over interest groups, Ruth Collier and David Collier make the distinction between "inducements" and "constraints." See Ruth Berins Collier and David Collier, "Inducements versus Constraints: Disaggregating 'Corporatism'," *American Political Science Review* 73, 4 (December 1979): 967–86.

13. Daniel Levy, "University Autonomy in Mexico: Implications for Regime Authoritarianism," *Latin American Research Review* 14, 3 (1979): 129–52; Susan Kaufman Purcell and John F. H. Purcell, "State and Society in Mexico: Must a Stable Polity Be Institutionalized?" *World Politics* 32, 2 (January 1980): 194–227; Dale Story, "Entrepreneurs and the State in Mexico: Examining the Authoritarian Thesis," *Technical Paper Series*, no. 30 (Austin: Institute of Latin American Studies, University of Texas, 1980); and Rose J. Spalding, "State Power and Its Limits: Corporatism in Mexico," *Comparative Political Studies* 14, 2 (July 1981): 139–61.

14. Frank R. Brandenburg, "Organized Business in Mexico," *Inter-American Economic Affairs* 12, 3 (Winter 1958): 36, 48–49; Raymond Vernon, *The Dilemma of Mexico's Development* (Cambridge, Mass.: Harvard University Press, 1963), p. 76; and Scott, *Mexican Government*, pp. 285–87. See also chapter 6 here.

15. On the human rights record of Mexico, see the annual publications of Amnesty International, *Amnesty International Report* (London: Amnesty International Publications) and of the U.S. Department of State, *Country Reports on Human Rights Practices* (Report Submitted to the Committee on Foreign Affairs, U.S. House of Representatives and to the Committee on Foreign Relations, U.S. Senate).

16. Prior to 1981 Mexico was even higher in its ranking on human rights, as four countries have moved past Mexico since then: Honduras (November 1981 elections), Bolivia (October 1982 civilian government), Brazil (November 1982 elections), and Argentina (December 1983 elections). See Raymond D. Gastil, "The Comparative Survey of Freedom 1985," *Freedom at Issue* no. 82 (January–February 1985): 3–15.

17. U.S. Department of State, *Country Reports for 1983* (February 1984), p. 624.

CHAPTER 2

1. Ronald H. McDonald, *Party Systems and Elections in Latin America* (Chicago: Markham Publishing Company, 1971), pp. 220–24.

2. Michael C. Meyer and William L. Sherman, *The Course of Mexican History* (New York: Oxford University Press, 1979), p. 324; and Levy and Székely, *Mexico*, p. 25.

3. Hansen, *Mexican Development*, p. 17.

4. The 1883 report is Fernando Rosenzweig, "La Industria," in Daniel Cosío

Villegas, ed., *Historia Moderna de México*, vol. 7, pt. 1, *El Porfiriato, La Vida Económica* (Mexico City: Editorial Hermes, 1965), pp. 311–481; and Dirección General de Estadística, *Estadística industrial formada por la Dirección General de Estadística a cargo del Dr. Antonio Peñafiel* (1903).

5. Ramón Eduardo Ruiz, *Labor and the Ambivalent Revolutionaries: Mexico, 1911–1923* (Baltimore: The Johns Hopkins University Press, 1976).

6. Dale Story, *Sectoral Clash and Industrialization in Latin America* (Syracuse, N.Y.: Maxwell School of Citizenship and Public Affairs, 1981), pp. 23–27.

7. Meyer and Sherman, *Mexican History*, p. 511.

8. Peter H. Smith, "La política dentro de la Revolución: El congreso constituyente de 1916–1917," *Historia Mexicana* 22, 3 (January–March 1973): 363–95.

9. Karl M. Schmitt, *Communism in Mexico: A Study in Political Frustration* (Austin: University of Texas Press, 1965), p. 4; and Hobart A. Spalding, Jr., *Organized Labor in Latin America* (New York: Harper and Row, 1977), pp. 104–105.

10. Robert Jones Shafer, *Mexican Business Organizations: History and Analysis* (Syracuse, N.Y.: Syracuse University Press, 1973), pp. 21–30.

11. Ibid., p. 22.

12. Pablo González Casanova, *El estado y los partidos políticos en México* (Mexico: Ediciones Era, 1983), p. 42; Octavio Rodríguez Araujo, *La reforma política y los partidos en México* (Mexico: Siglo Veintiuno Editores, 1983), pp. 27–28; and Luis Javier Garrido, *El partido de la revolución institucionalizada: la formación del nuevo estado en México (1928–1945)* (Mexico: Siglo Veintiuno Editores, 1984), pp. 37–55.

13. Rodríguez Araujo, *La reforma política*, pp. 29–30.

14. Scott, *Mexican Government*, p. 124.

15. Portes Gile was still quite subordinate to Calles, however. For example, after Calles put his son Alfredo in the state legislature of Tamaulipas, Portes Gil was quoted as complaining that "General Calles was not satisfied that his sons Rodolfo and Plutarco governed Sonora and Nuevo León. He also wanted Tamaulipas under the thumb of the family." Scott, *Mexican Government*, p. 123.

CHAPTER 3

1. James W. Wilkie, *The Mexican Revolution: Federal Expenditures and Social Change since 1910* (Berkeley: University of California Press, 1967), pp. 102–103.

2. See Dale Story, "Policy Cycles in Mexican Presidential Politics," *Latin American Research Review*, forthcoming.

3. Martin C. Needler, *Politics and Society in Mexico* (Albuquerque: University of New Mexico Press, 1971), p. 47.

4. Grindle, "Policy Change," p. 525.

5. E. V. K. Fitzgerald, "Patterns of Public Sector Income and Expenditure in Mexico," Technical Papers Series, no. 17 (Austin: Institute of Latin American Studies, University of Texas, 1978), p. 3.

6. Harvey Kaye, "How 'New' Is Mexico's Foreign Policy?" *Inter-American Economic Affairs* 28, 4 (Spring 1975): 90; and William Hamilton, "Mexico's 'New' Foreign Policy: A Reexamination," *Inter-American Economic Affairs* 29, 3 (Winter 1975): 53.

7. The first evidence was presented in David Gordon, "Mexico: A Survey," *The Economist*, April 22, 1978, p. 16. For a more detailed examination of the data, see Story, "Policy Cycles."

8. See Evelyn P. Stevens, *Protest and Response in Mexico* (Cambridge, Mass.: MIT Press, 1974), pp. 99–126.

9. One of the major demands of the student protestors was to disband the *granderos* corps, which had been created in 1944 by Avila Camacho in order to put down a strike in a munitions factory.

10. For a summary and generally positive interpretation of Echeverría's spending policies, see Carlos Tello Macías, *La política económica en México 1970–1976* (Mexico: Editorial Siglo Veintiuno, 1979). Also see Norris Clement and Louis Green, "The Political Economy of Devaluation in Mexico," *Inter-American Economic Affairs* 32, 3 (Winter 1978): 47–75.

11. Smith, *Labyrinths*, p. 280.

12. Martin C. Needler, *Mexican Politics: The Containment of Conflict* (New York: Praeger, 1982), p. 36; and Kenneth F. Johnson, *Mexican Democracy: A Critical View* (New York: Praeger, 1978), pp. 51–52, 97–107. Johnson suggests that Echeverría not only knew of but approved of *Los Halcones*.

13. Levy and Székely, *Mexico*, p. 36.

14. See "Discurso de Toma de Posesión de Miguel de la Madrid Hurtado," *El Día*, December 2, 1982; and "Mensaje a la nación," *Comercio Exterior*, December 1982.

15. See Ernest A. Duff, *Leader and Party in Latin America* (Boulder, Colo.: Westview Press, 1984). Duff includes Betancourt in Venezuela, Trujillo in the Dominican Republic, along with Calles in Mexico as the most successful builders of party institutions in the region.

CHAPTER 4

1. Calles in 1924 received the lowest vote total (84 percent) of any president before 1946.

2. Comisión Federal Electoral, *Reforma Política: Memoria del Proceso Federal Electoral 1981–82*, vol. 10 (Mexico: Secretaría Técnica, 1982), p. 5.

3. See Kevin J. Middlebrook, "Political Change in Mexico," in Susan Kaufman Purcell, ed., *Mexico–United States Relations* (New York: The Academy of Political Science, 1981), pp. 55–66; and Kevin J. Middlebrook, *Political Liberalization in an Authoritarian Regime: The Case of Mexico* (La Jolla, Cal.: Center for U.S.–Mexican Studies, University of California, San Diego, 1985).

4. Comisión Federal Electoral, *Reforma Política*, vol. 10, p. 12.

5. Since 1973 parties had to demonstrate the existence of at least 65,000 members nationwide with 2,000 or more members located in each of at least two-thirds of the 31 states. With the addition of the substantial bureaucratic obstacles, registration became an impossible task for most parties. See Johnson, *Mexican Democracy*, p. 150.

6. Interviews, December 1984.

7. Franz A. von Sauer, *The Alienated "Loyal" Opposition: Mexico's Partido Ac-*

ción Nacional (Albuquerque: University of New Mexico Press, 1974), pp. 15, 45–60.

8. Rodríguez Araujo, *La reforma política*, p. 126. González Casanova, *El estado*, p. 78, says that the PAN was formed partly by old *maderistas*.

9. Donald J. Mabry, *Mexico's Acción Nacional: A Catholic Alternative to Revolution* (Syracuse, N.Y.: Syracuse University Press, 1973), pp. 32–33.

10. Partido Acción Nacional, *Cambio democrático de estructura* (Mexico: Editores de Acción Nacional, 1969). The reference to political humanism is from Johnson, *Mexican Democracy*, p. 144. In his 1978 book Johnson practically apologizes for his earlier descriptions of the PAN as a "distinctly reactionary or right-wing party." In fact, he describes some of the PAN leaders as being "quite progressive."

11. Partido Acción Nacional, *Nuestros Ideales: Principios de Doctrina* (Mexico: Ediciones PAN, 1984). Also see José Angel Conchello et al., *Los partidos políticos de México* (Mexico: Fondo de Cultura Económica, 1975), pp. 11–144.

12. Partido Acción Nacional, *Cambio*, p. 14.

13. Rodríguez Araujo, *La reforma política*, p. 126.

14. Mabry, *Acción Nacional*, p. 43.

15. In particular, see John Walton and Joyce A. Sween, "Urbanization, Industrialization and Voting in Mexico: A Longitudinal Analysis of Official and Opposition Party Support," *Social Science Quarterly* 52, 3 (December 1971): 721–45; Rafael Segovia, "Las elecciones federales de 1979," *Foro Internacional* 20, 3 (1980): 397–410; and Joseph L. Klesner, "Party System Expansion and Electoral Mobilization in Mexico" (Paper delivered at the XII International Congress of the Latin American Studies Association, Albuquerque, New Mexico, April 18–20, 1985). Another source of electoral analysis is Pablo González Casanova, ed., *Las elecciones en México: evolución y perspectivas* (Mexico: Siglo Veintiuno Editores, 1985).

16. The sources for these data are Nacional Financiera, *La economía Mexicana en cifras 1984* (Mexico: Nacional Financiera, 1984), pp. 26–29; and Secretaría de Programación y Presupuesto, *X Censo General de Población y Vivienda, 1980* (Mexico: Instituto Nacional de Estadística, Geografía e Informática, 1984), pp. 9–11, 75–98.

17. Schmitt, *Communism*, p. 19.

18. Levy and Székely, *Mexico*, p. 75.

19. The issue of which party is more "extremist" is a debatable point. Needler, *Mexican Politics*, p. 67, suggests that PDM is the more moderate of the two—favoring a "populist" focus on the poor. On the other hand, Levy and Székely, *Mexico*, p. 76, say the PDM's ideology is to the right of that of the PAN and that the PDM is the most overtly conservative party in Mexico.

20. The Federal District is essentially Mexico City; the state of México includes most of the metropolitan surroundings of Mexico City; Jalisco contains Guadalajara, the nation's second largest city; and Baja California includes Tijuana and Mexicali, two of the largest border cities. The PRI also did not fare well in Monterrey, Nuevo León—the third major metropolitan area of Mexico.

21. Kenneth M. Coleman, *Diffuse Support in Mexico: The Potential for Crisis* (Beverly Hills, Cal.: Sage Publications, 1976).

22. Roderic A. Camp and Miguel A. Basañez, "The Nationalizations of Banks and Mexican Public Opinion," *The Mexican Forum*, 4, 2 (April 1984): 1–8.

23. This poll was conducted by the publications *Contenido* and *El Norte* and reported in *The Mexican Forum* 4, 2 (April 1984): 17.

24. The same conclusion was reached in 1970 by Barry Ames, "Bases of Support for Mexico's Dominant Party," *American Political Science Review* 64 (March 1970): 153–67.

25. U.S. Department of State, *Country Reports for 1983*, p. 624.

26. Levy and Székely, *Mexico*, p. 68.

27. One useful case study of electoral fraud in the state of Sonora and of the manipulation by the PRI through handpicking its candidates is found in Johnson, *Mexican Democracy*, pp. 179–94.

28. *Wall Street Journal*, January 12, 1984, and March 21, 1984.

CHAPTER 5

1. Partido Revolucionario Institucional, *Documentos Básicos; Declaración de Principios, Programa de Acción, y Estatutos* (Mexico: Comité Ejecutivo Nacional, Partido Revolucionario Institucional, 1984), pp. 135–36.

2. Ibid., pp. 156–216. Other sources for information on party organization are Robert K. Furtak, *El Partido de la Revolución y la estabilidad política en México* (Mexico: Universidad Nacional Autónoma de México, 1978), pp. 79–92; and Scott, *Mexican Government*, pp. 154–61.

3. The Twelfth National Assembly of the PRI met in August of 1984 with some 6,000 Party members in attendance and almost 2,000 official delegates. The delegates were distributed as follows: 158 from the National Executive Committee, 314 from the agrarian sector, 516 from the labor sector, 290 from the popular sector, 100 from the youth group, 132 from the women's affiliate, 64 senators, and 299 deputies. See Partido Revolucionario Institucional, XII Asamblea Nacional, *Memoria, Tres Jornadas de Trabajo*, vol. 2 (Mexico: Comité Ejecutivo Nacional, Partido Revolucionario Institucional, 1984), p. 143.

4. Emilio Portes Gil and Lázaro Cárdenas served as president of the CEN. Adolfo López Mateos served as secretary-general of the CEN.

5. Partido Revolucionario Institucional, *Documentos Básicos*, p. 189.

6. Instituto de Estudios Políticos, Económicos y Sociales, Partido Revolucionario Institucional, *Plan Básico 1982–1988 y Plataforma Electoral* (Mexico: Partido Revolucionario Institucional, 1981).

7. John F. H. Purcell and Susan Kaufman Purcell, "Machine Politics and Socio-economic Change in Mexico," in James W. Wilkie, Michael C. Meyer, and Edna Monzón de Wilkie, eds., *Contemporary Mexico: Papers of the IV International Congress of Mexican History* (Berkeley: University of California Press, 1976), pp. 353–54.

8. Hansen, *Mexican Development*, pp. 107–22.

9. See Mancur Olson, *The Logic of Collective Action: Public Goods and the Theory of Groups* (Cambridge, Mass.: Harvard University Press, 1971).

10. For a case study analyzing PRI involvement in two lower-income urban areas, see Susan Eckstein, "The State and the Urban Poor," in José Luis Reyna

and Richard S. Weinert, eds., *Authoritarianism in Mexico* (Philadelphia: Institute for the Study of Human Issues, 1977), pp. 23–46.

11. As one example, the profit-sharing clause of the 1917 Constitution was not put into effect until the early 1960s.

12. Spalding, *Organized Labor*, p. 103.

13. Rodríguez Araujo, *La reforma política*, p. 26.

14. Spalding, *Organized Labor*, pp. 113–14.

15. See Kenneth M. Coleman and Charles L. Davis, "Preemptive Reform and the Mexican Working Class," *Latin American Research Review* 18, 1 (1983): 3–31.

16. Roderic A. Camp, "Organized Labor and the Mexican State: A Symbiotic Relationship?" *The Mexican Forum* 4, 4 (October 1984): 6–7.

17. Ibid., p. 5.

18. For one account of the degree of corruption throughout Mexico, see Alan Riding, *Distant Neighbors: A Portrait of the Mexicans* (New York: Alfred A. Knopf, 1985), pp. 113–33.

19. *Wall Street Journal*, January 6, 1984.

20. Howard Handelman, "Unionization, Ideology, and Political Participation within the Mexican Working Class," in Mitchell A. Seligson and John A. Booth, eds., *Political Participation in Latin America*, Vol. 2: *Politics and the Poor* (New York: Holmes and Meier, 1979), p. 154.

21. Yet at the Twelfth National Assembly of the PRI in 1985, representation of the agrarian sector was only 60 percent as large as the labor sector delegation. On the estimates of number of members in the three sectors, see Furtak, *El Partido*, p. 92.

22. Ibid., pp. 66–67.

23. Rosa Elena Montes de Oca, "The State and the Peasants," in José Luis Reyna and Richard S. Weinert, eds., *Authoritarianism in Mexico* (Philadelphia: Institute for the Study of Human Issues, 1977), pp. 49–50.

24. Spalding, *Organized Labor*, pp. 110–11.

25. The greatest threat to PRI monopoly over peasant support has been the UNS, which has attracted those peasants who are motivated more by religious convictions.

26. Montes de Oca, "The State and Peasants," p. 55.

27. Ibid., p. 58.

28. Johnson, *Mexican Democracy*, pp. 158–66.

29. One estimate says it is almost 300,000 members less than the labor sector and 800,000 less than the agrarian sector. See Furtak, *El Partido*, p. 92. Its delegation to the PRI's Twelfth National Assembly in 1984 was the smallest sectoral representation and was just over half the size of the labor delegation.

30. Even the label "popular" may be a misnomer, though it is a direct translation from the Spanish adjective officially used by the PRI to describe this sector.

31. Furtak, *El Partido*, pp. 70–71, 92.

32. Camp, "Organized Labor," p. 3.

33. Ibid., p. 3.

34. L. Vincent Padgett, *The Mexican Political System* (Boston: Houghton Mifflin, 1966), p. 125.

CHAPTER 6

1. Edwin Lieuwen, "Depoliticization of the Mexican Revolutionary Army, 1915–1940," in David Ronfeldt, ed., *The Modern Mexican Military: A Reassessment* (La Jolla, Cal.: Center for U.S.-Mexican Studies, University of California, San Diego, 1984), pp. 51–61.

2. Scott, *Mexican Government*, p. 134.

3. Levy and Székely, *Mexico*, p. 40.

4. For an elaboration of this theme, see Ronfeldt, ed., *The Modern Mexican Military*.

5. Ibid., pp. 3, 170–71.

6. Robert N. Pierce, *Keeping the Flame: Media and Government in Latin America* (New York: Hastings House, 1979), p. 106.

7. Ibid., p. 107.

8. Ibid., pp. 105–106.

9. Comisión Federal Electoral, *Reforma Política*, vol. 9, p. 92.

10. *The Dallas Morning News*, November 5, 1984.

11. Elizabeth Mahan, "Who Controls? Broadcast Industry–State Interactions in Mexico," *The Mexican Forum* 3, 3 (July 1983): 9–10.

12. Echeverría has been unique among former presidents in maintaining important political and economic ties throughout Mexico.

13. Marvin Alisky, *Latin American Media: Guidance and Censorship* (Ames: Iowa State University Press, 1981), pp. 9, 46, 59–62.

14. See ibid., pp. 51–63; and Mahan, "Who Controls?," pp. 9–10.

15. Alisky, *Latin American Media*, p. 52.

16. Johnson, *Mexican Democracy*, pp. 156–62.

17. Actually, PIPSA rarely employs its power to deny its newsprint to a publication. The only previous known instance occurred in 1968 when the Marxist news magazine *Política* ceased publishing after PIPSA suspended its supply of paper. See Alisky, *Latin American Media*, pp. 38–39.

18. Two of the best accounts of the *Excélsior* case are Levy and Székely, *Mexico*, pp. 94–99, and Pierce, *Keeping the Flame*, pp. 115–18.

19. Reliance upon a government-dominated labor union to pressure a newspaper was not a new strategy. An independent regional paper, *El ABC de Tijuana*, was purged in a similar fashion. See Levy and Székely, *Mexico*, pp. 93–94.

20. *Dallas Times Herald*, November 16, 1984.

21. Pierce, *Keeping the Flame*, p. 113.

22. Kim Quaile Hill and Patricia A. Hurley, "Freedom of the Press in Latin America: A Thirty-Year Survey," *Latin American Research Review* 15, 2 (1980): 212–18.

23. Much of this discussion of the private sector comes from Dale Story, *Industry, the State, and Public Policy in Mexico* (Austin: University of Texas Press, 1986), chap. 4. See also William Glade, "Mexico: Party-Led Development," in Robert Wesson, ed., *Politics, Policies, and Economic Development in Latin America* (Stanford, Cal.: Hoover Institution Press, 1984), pp. 97–99.

24. Personal interviews, June 1979.

25. John F. H. Purcell and Susan Kaufman Purcell, "Mexican Business and Public Policy," in James M. Malloy, ed., *Authoritarianism and Corporatism in Latin America* (Pittsburgh: University of Pittsburgh Press, 1977), p. 194–95; and Shafer, *Mexican Business Organizations*, pp. 54–58, 67–70, and 107–12.

26. Ibid., p. 107.

27. For a case study of CANACINTRA's successful opposition to Mexico's planned entry into the GATT, see Dale Story, "Trade Politics in the Third World: A Case Study of the Mexican GATT Decision," *International Organization* 36, 4 (Autumn 1982): 767–94.

28. Shafer, *Mexican Business Organizations*, p. 56; and personal interviews, June 1979.

29. Miguel Basáñez, *La lucha por la hegemonía en México* (Mexico: Siglo Veintiuno Editores, 1982), pp. 81–84, 98–102, and 210.

30. Flavia Derossi, *The Mexican Entrepreneur* (Paris: Development Centre of the Organisation for Economic Co-operation and Development, 1971), p. 61; Peter H. Smith, "Does Mexico Have a Power Elite?," in José Luis Reyna and Richard S. Weinert, eds., *Authoritarianism in Mexico* (Philadelphia: Institute for the Study of Human Issues, 1977), pp. 129–51; and Dale Story, "Industrial Elites in Mexico: Political Ideology and Influence," *Journal of Interamerican Studies and World Affairs* 25, 3 (August 1983): 351–76.

CHAPTER 7

1. Eckstein, "State and Urban Poor," pp. 28–30.

2. Ibid., p. 29.

3. Roderic A. Camp, *Mexico's Leaders: Their Education and Recruitment* (Tucson: University of Arizona Press, 1980), pp. 18–24. Also see Merilee Serrill Grindle, *Bureaucrats, Politicians, and Peasants in Mexico: A Case Study in Public Policy* (Berkeley: University of California Press, 1977); and Larissa Lomnitz, "Horizontal and Vertical Relations and the Social Structure of Urban Mexico," *Latin American Research Review* 17, 2 (1982): 51–74.

4. Johnson, *Mexican Democracy*, pp. 84–87; and Smith, *Labyrinths*, pp. 250–51.

5. Smith, *Labyrinths*, p. 227.

6. For example, the cabinet played a crucial role in the 1980 decision not to join the GATT. See Story, "Trade Politics," p. 787.

7. Johnson, *Mexican Democracy*, pp. 57–58. For further information on the presidential succession process, see Evelyn P. Stevens, "The Mexican Presidential Succession," *Journal of Interamerican Studies and World Affairs* 19, 1 (February 1977): 125–26; and Steven E. Sanderson, "Presidential Succession and Political Rationality in Mexico," *World Politics* 35, 3 (April 1983): 315–34.

8. Instituto de Estudios Políticos, Económicos y Sociales, Partido Revolucionario Institucional, *Plan Básico*.

9. *Diario Oficial*, January 5, 1983.

10. John Bailey has described how the *técnicos* in Programming and Budget have replaced the Party *políticos* in formulating six-year plans. See John J. Bailey, "Presidency, Bureaucracy, and Administrative Reform in Mexico: The Sec-

retariat of Programming and Budget," *Inter-American Economic Affairs* 34, 1 (Summer 1980): 27–60.

11. In particular, see Smith, *Labyrinths*, pp. 133–58. Smith actually identifies three separate paths, which he labels the "electoral" track (principally local officials and federal deputies), the "administrative" track (primarily heads of the mid-level and semiautonomous agencies), and the "executive" track (the president, cabinet, and subcabinet). For our purposes, we are focusing on the first and last tracks.

12. Needler, *Mexican Politics*, p. 80.

13. See Camp, *Mexico's Leaders*; Roderic A. Camp, "Technocracy, Representation, and Criticism: Mexico in the Next Six Years," *Mexican Forum*, special issue (December 1982), pp. 23–25; and Needler, *Mexican Politics*, pp. 80–81.

14. Daniel Levy, *University and Government in Mexico: Autonomy in an Authoritarian System* (New York: Praeger, 1980).

15. Smith, *Labyrinths*, pp. 85, 114, 130, 298–302, 306.

16. In her case study of CONASUPO, Merilee Grindle downplays the distinctions between *técnicos* and *políticos*. See Merilee S. Grindle, "Power, Expertise and the 'Técnico': Suggestions from a Mexican Case Study," *The Journal of Politics* 39, 2 (May 1977): 399–426.

17. See Roderic A. Camp, "The Middle-Level Technocrat in Mexico," *The Journal of Developing Areas* 6, 4 (July 1972): 571–82.

18. López Mateos came from the Ministry of Labor, López Portillo from Finance, and de la Madrid from Programming and Budget.

19. A number of presidents did manage the presidential campaigns of their predecessors. Besides López Mateos, Alemán headed the Avila Camacho campaign in 1940, and Ruiz Cortines did the same for Alemán in 1946. López Portillo worked in the campaign of López Mateos in 1958, though not in a top-ranking post.

20. Reyes Heroles (second oldest cabinet member—born in 1921) and Salinas de Gortari (youngest cabinet member—born in 1948) provide an interesting contrast. Besides their age differences, Reyes Heroles was the only example of a *político* in the cabinet, while Salinas de Gortari was probably the most extreme *técnico*. Also, Reyes Heroles had arguably the fewest ties to de la Madrid, while Salinas de Gortari had been one of de la Madrid's closest advisors.

CHAPTER 8

1. In addition to the quote included here, several scholars refer to the "crisis of the eighties" and the "social volcano" in Mexico. See Jim Cockroft and Ross Gandy, "The Mexican Volcano," *Monthly Review* 33, 1 (May 1981): 32–44; Donald Hodges and Ross Gandy, *Mexico 1910–1976: Reform or Revolution?* (London: Zed Press, 1979); and Judith Adler Hellman, *Mexico in Crisis* (New York: Holmes and Meier, 1983).

2. See Robert R. Kaufman, "Mexico and Latin American Authoritarianism," in José Luis Reyna and Richard S. Weinert, eds. *Authoritarianism in Mexico* (Philadelphia: Institute for the Study of Human Issues, 1977), pp. 193–232.

3. Story, "Policy Cycles."

4. One of the most obvious examples of manipulating foreign policy to

counteract domestic pressures from the left was provided by the Echeverría administration. Precisely to rid himself of the "stigma of Tlatelolco" Echeverría took Mexico's foreign policy further to the left than any president since Cárdenas. See Yoram Shapira, *Mexican Foreign Policy Under Echeverría*, The Washington Papers, vol. 6, no. 56 (Beverly Hills, Cal.: Sage Publications, 1978).

5. Along these same lines, Steven Sanderson argues that another challenge for the PRI is to restore the "old-style populism." See Steven E. Sanderson, "Political Tensions in the Mexican Party System," *Current History* 82, 488 (December 1983): 401–405.

Bibliography

Alisky, Marvin. *Latin American Media: Guidance and Censorship*. Ames: Iowa State University Press, 1981.

Ames, Barry. "Bases of Support for Mexico's Dominant Party." *American Political Science Review* 64 (March 1970): 153–67.

Amnesty International. *Amnesty International Report* various years. London: Amnesty International Publications.

Bailey, John J. "Presidency, Bureaucracy, and Administrative Reform in Mexico: The Secretariat of Programming and Budget." *Inter-American Economic Affairs* 34, 1 (Summer 1980): 27–60.

Basáñez, Miguel. *La lucha por la hegemonía en México*. Mexico: Siglo Veintiuno Editores, 1982.

Booth, John A. and Seligson, Mitchell A. "The Political Culture of Authoritarianism in Mexico: A Reexamination." *Latin American Research Review* 19, 1 (1984): 106–24.

Brandenburg, Frank R. "Organized Business in Mexico." *Inter-American Economic Affairs* 12, 3 (Winter 1958): 26–50.

Camp, Roderic A. *Mexican Political Biographies, 1935–1975*. Tucson: University of Arizona Press, 1976.

Camp, Roderic A. *Mexico's Leaders: Their Education and Recruitment*. Tucson: University of Arizona Press, 1980.

Camp, Roderic A. "The Middle–Level Technocrat in Mexico." *The Journal of Developing Areas* 6, 4 (July 1972): 571–82.

Camp, Roderic A. "Organized Labor and the Mexican State: A Symbiotic Relationship?" *The Mexican Forum* 4, 4 (October 1984): 6–7.

Camp, Roderic A. "Technocracy, Representation, and Criticism: Mexico in the Next Six Years." *Mexican Forum* special issue (December 1982): 23–25.

Camp, Roderic A. and Basáñez, Miguel A. "The Natonalizations of Banks and Mexican Public Opinion." *The Mexican Forum* 4, 2 (April 1984): 1–8.

Clement, Norris and Green, Louis. "The Political Economy of Devaluation in Mexico." *Inter-American Economic Affairs* 32, 3 (Winter 1978): 47–75.

Cockroft, James. *El imperialismo, la lucha de clases y el estado en México*. Mexico: Editorial Nuestro Tiempo, 1980.

Cockroft, James D. *Mexico: Class Formation, Capital Accumulation, and the State*. New York: Monthly Review Press, 1983.

Cockroft, Jim and Gandy, Ross. "The Mexican Volcano." *Monthly Review* 33, 1 (May 1981): 32–44.

Coleman, Kenneth M. *Diffuse Support in Mexico: The Potential for Crisis.* Beverly Hills, Cal.: Sage Publications, 1976.

Coleman, Kenneth M. and Davis, Charles L. "Preemptive Reform and the Mexican Working Class." *Latin American Research Review* 18, 1 (1983): 3–31.

Collier, Ruth Berins and Collier, David. "Inducements versus Constraints: Disaggregating 'Corporatism'." *American Political Science Review* 73, 4 (December 1979): 976–86.

Comisión Federal Electoral. *Reforma Política: Memoria del Proceso Federal Electoral 1981–82,* vols. 9–10. Mexico: Secretaría Técnica, 1982.

Conchello, José Angel, et al. *Los partidos políticos de México.* Mexico: Fondo de Cultura Económica, 1975.

Derossi, Flavia. *The Mexican Entrepreneur.* Paris: Development Centre of the Organisation for Economic Co-operation and Development, 1971.

Dirección General de Estadística. *Estadística industrial formada por la Dirección General de Estadística a cargo del Dr. Antonio Peñafiel.* 1903.

Duff, Ernest A. *Leader and Party in Latin America.* Boulder, Colo.: Westview Press, 1984.

Eckstein, Susan. "The State and the Urban Poor." In José Luis Reyna and Richard S. Weinert, eds., *Authoritarianism in Mexico.* Philadelphia: Institute for the Study of Human Issues, 1977, pp. 23–46.

Fitzgerald, E. V. K. "Patterns of Public Sector Income and Expenditure in Mexico." *Technical Papers Series,* no. 17. Austin: Institute of Latin American Studies, University of Texas, 1978.

Furtak, Robert K. *El Partido de la Revolución y la estabilidad política en México.* Mexico: Universidad Nacional Autónoma de México, 1978.

Garrido, Luis Javier. *El partido de la revolución institucionalizada: la formación del nuevo estado en México (1928–1945).* Mexico: Siglo Veintiuno Editores, 1984.

Gastil, Raymond D. "The Comparative Survey of Freedom 1985." *Freedom at Issue,* no. 82 (January–February 1985): 3–15.

Glade, William. "Mexico: Party-Led Development." In Robert Wesson, ed., *Politics, Policies, and Economic Development in Latin America.* Stanford, Cal.: Hoover Institution Press, 1984, pp. 94–123.

González Casanova, Pablo. *Democracy in Mexico.* New York: Oxford University Press, 1970.

González Casanova, Pablo. *El estado y los partidos políticos en México.* Mexico: Ediciones Era, 1983.

González Casanova, Pablo, ed. *Las elecciones en México: evolución y perspectivas.* Mexico: Siglo Veintiuno Editores, 1985.

Gordon, David. "Mexico: A Survey." *The Economist,* April 22, 1978, pp. 15–17.

Grindle, Merilee Serrill. *Bureaucrats, Politicians and Peasants in Mexico: A Case Study in Public Policy.* Berkeley: University of California Press, 1977.

Grindle, Merilee S. "Policy Change in an Authoritarian Regime: Mexico under Echeverría." *Journal of Interamerican Studies and World Affairs* 19, 4 (November 1977): 523–55.

Grindle, Merilee S. "Power, Expertise, and the 'Técnico': Suggestions from a Mexican Case Study." *The Journal of Politics* 39, 2 (May 1977): 399–426.

Hamilton, Nora. *The Limits of State Autonomy: Post-Revolutionary Mexico*. Princeton, N.J.: Princeton University Press, 1982.

Hamilton, William. "Mexico's 'New' Foreign Policy: A Reexamination." *Inter-American Economic Affairs* 29, 3 (Winter 1975): 51–58.

Handelman, Howard. "Unionization, Ideology, and Political Participation within the Mexican Working Class." In Mitchell A. Seligson and John A. Booth, eds., *Political Participation in Latin America, Volume II: Politics and the Poor*. New York: Holmes and Meier, 1979, pp. 154–68.

Hansen, Roger D. *The Politics of Mexican Development*. Baltimore: The Johns Hopkins University Press, 1974.

Hellman, Judith Adler. *Mexico in Crisis*. New York: Holmes and Meier, 1983.

Hill, Kim Quaile and Hurley, Patricia A. "Freedom of the Press in Latin America: A Thirty-Year Survey." *Latin American Research Review* 15, 2 (1980): 212–18.

Hodges, Donald and Gandy, Ross. *Mexico 1910–1976: Reform or Revolution?* London: Zed Press, 1979.

Instituto de Estudios Políticos, Económicos, y Sociales, Partido Revolucionario Institucional. *Plan Básico 1982–1988 y Plataforma Electoral*. Mexico: Partido Revolucionario Institucional, 1981.

Johnson, Kenneth F. *Mexican Democracy: A Critical View*. New York: Praeger, 1978.

Kaufman, Robert R. "Mexico and Latin American Authoritarianism." In José Luis Reyna and Richard S. Weinert, eds., *Authoritarianism in Mexico*. Philadelphia: Institute for the Study of Human Issues, 1977, pp. 193–232.

Kaye, Harvey. "How 'New' Is Mexico's Foreign Policy?" *Inter-American Economic Affairs* 28, 4 (Spring 1975): 87–92.

Klesner, Joseph L. "Party System Expansion and Electoral Mobilization in Mexico." Paper delivered at the XII International Congress of the Latin American Studies Association, Albuquerque, New Mexico, April 18–20, 1985.

Levy, Daniel. "University Autonomy in Mexico: Implications for Regime Authoritarianism." *Latin American Research Review* 14, 3 (1979): 129–52.

Levy, Daniel. *University and Government in Mexico: Autonomy in an Authoritarian System*. New York: Praeger, 1980.

Levy, Daniel and Székely, Gabriel. *Mexico: Paradoxes of Stability and Change*. Boulder, Colo.: Westview Press, 1983.

Lieuwen, Edwin. "Depoliticization of the Mexican Revolutionary Army, 1915–1940." In David Ronfeldt, ed., *The Modern Mexican Military: A Reassessment*. La Jolla, Cal.: Center for U.S.-Mexican Studies, University of California, San Diego, 1984, pp. 51–61.

Linz, Juan J. "An Authoritarian Regime: The Case of Spain." In Erik Allardt and Stein Rokkan, eds., *Mass Politics: Studies in Political Sociology*. New York: Free Press, 1970, pp. 251–83.

Lomnitz, Larissa. "Horizontal and Vertical Relations and the Social Structure of Urban Mexico." *Latin American Research Review* 17, 2 (1982): 51–74.

Mabry, Donald J. *Mexico's Acción Nacional: A Catholic Alternative to Revolution*. Syracuse, N.Y.: Syracuse University Press, 1973.

Mahan, Elizabeth. "Who Controls? Broadcast Industry–State Interactions in Mexico." *The Mexican Forum* 3, 3 (July 1983): 9–10.

McDonald, Ronald H. *Party Systems and Elections in Latin America.* Chicago: Markham Publishing Company, 1971.

Meyer, Michael C. and Sherman, William L. *The Course of Mexican History.* New York: Oxford University Press, 1979.

Middlebrook, Kevin J. "Political Change in Mexico." In Susan Kaufman Purcell, ed., *Mexico–United States Relations.* New York: The Academy of Political Science, 1981, pp. 55–66.

Middlebrook, Kevin J. *Political Liberalization in an Authoritarian Regime: The Case of Mexico.* La Jolla, Cal.: Center for U.S.-Mexican Studies, University of California, San Diego, 1985.

Montes de Oca, Rosa Elena. "The State and the Peasants." In José Luis Reyna and Richard S. Weinert, eds., *Authoritarianism in Mexico.* Philadelphia: Institute for the Study of Human Issues, 1977, pp. 47–66.

Nacional Financiera. *La economía Mexicana en cifras 1984.* Mexico: Nacional Financiera, 1984.

Needler, Martin C. *Mexican Politics: The Containment of Conflict.* New York: Praeger, 1982.

Needler, Martin C. *Politics and Society in Mexico.* Albuquerque: University of New Mexico Press, 1971.

Olson, Mancur. *The Logic of Collective Action: Public Goods and the Theory of Groups.* Cambridge, Mass.: Harvard University Press, 1971.

Padgett, L. Vincent. *The Mexican Political System.* Boston: Houghton Mifflin, 1966.

Partido Acción Nacional. *Cambio democrático de estructura.* Mexico: Editores de Acción Nacional, 1969.

Partido Acción Nacional. *Nuestros Ideales: Pricipios de Doctrina.* Mexico: Ediciones PAN, 1984.

Partido Revolucionario Institucional. *Documentos Básicos: Declaracion de Principios, Programa de Acción, y Estatutos.* Mexico: Comité Ejecutivo Nacional, Partido Revolucionario Institucional, 1984.

Partido Revolucionario Institucional, XII Asamblea Nacional. *Memoria, Tres Jornadas de Trabajo,* vol. 2. Mexico: Comité Ejecutivo Nacional, Partido Revolucionario Institucional, 1984.

Pierce, Robert N. *Keeping the Flame: Media and Government in Latin America.* New York: Hastings House, 1979.

Purcell, John F. H. and Purcell, Susan Kaufman. "Machine Politics and Socioeconomic Change in Mexico." In James W. Wilkie, Michael C. Meyer, and Edna Monzón de Wilkie, eds., *Contemporary Mexico: Papers of the IV International Congress of Mexican History.* Berkeley: University of California Press, 1976, pp. 348–66.

Purcell, John F. H. and Purcell, Susan Kaufman. "Mexican Business and Public Policy." In James M. Malloy, ed., *Authoritarianism and Corporatism in Latin America.* Pittsburgh: University of Pittsburgh Press, 1977, pp. 191–226.

Purcell, Susan Kaufman. "Business-Government Relations in Mexico: The Case of the Sugar Industry." *Comparative Politics* 13, 2 (January 1981): 211–33.

Purcell, Susan Kaufman. "Decision-Making in an Authoritarian Regime: Theoretical Implications from a Mexican Case Study." *World Politics* 26, 1 (October 1973): 28–54.

Purcell, Susan Kaufman. *The Mexican Profit-Sharing Decision: Politics in an Authoritarian Regime.* Berkeley: University of California Press, 1975.

Purcell, Susan Kaufman and Purcell, John F. H. "State and Society in Mexico: Must a Stable Polity Be Institutionalized?" *World Politics* 32, 2 (January 1980): 194–227.

Reyna, Josæ Luis and Weinert, Richard S., eds. *Authoritarianism in Mexico.* Philadelphia: Institute for the Study of Human Issues, 1977.

Riding, Alan. *Distant Neighbors: A Portrait of the Mexicans.* New York: Alfred A. Knopf, 1985.

Rodríguez Araujo, Octavio. *La reforma política y los partidos en México.* Mexico: Siglo Veintiuno Editores, 1983.

Rondfeldt, David, ed. *The Modern Mexican Military: A Reassessment.* La Jolla, Cal.: Center for U.S.-Mexican Studies, University of Califiornia, San Diego, 1984.

Rosenzweig, Fernando. "La Industria." In Daniel Cosío Villegas, ed., *Historia Moderna de México*, vol. 7, pt. 1, *El Porfiriato, La Vida Económica*. Mexico: Editorial Hermes, 1965, pp. 311–481.

Ruiz, Ramón Eduardo. *Labor and the Ambivalent Revolutionaries: Mexico, 1911–1923.* Baltimore: The Johns Hopkins University Press, 1976.

Sanderson, Steven E. "Political Tensions in the Mexican Party System." *Current History* 82, 488 (December 1983): 401–405.

Sanderson, Steven E. "Presidential Succession and Political Rationality in Mexico." *World Politics* 35, 3 (April 1983): 315–34.

Schmitt, Karl M. *Communism in Mexico: A Study in Political Frustration.* Austin: University of Texas Press, 1965.

Schmitter, Philippe C. "Still the Century of Corporatism?" *The Review of Politics* 36, 1 (January 1974): 85–131.

Scott, Robert E. *Mexican Government in Transition.* Urbana: University of Illinois Press, 1964.

Secretaría de Programación y Presupuesto. *X Censo General de Población y Vivienda, 1980.* Mexico: Instituto Nacional de Estadística, Geografía e Informática, 1984.

Segovia, Rafael. "Las elecciones federales de 1979." *Foro Internacional* 20, 3 (1980): 397–410.

Shafer, Robert Jones. *Mexican Business Organizations: History and Analysis.* Syracuse, N.Y.: Syracuse University Press, 1973.

Shapira, Yoram. *Mexican Foreign Policy Under Echeverría.* The Washington Papers, vol. 6, no. 56. Beverly Hills, Cal.: Sage Publications, 1978.

Smith, Peter H. "Does Mexico Have a Power Elite?" In José Luis Reyna and Richard S. Weinert, eds., *Authoritarianism in Mexico.* Philadelphia: Institute for the Study of Human Issues, 1977, pp. 129–51.

Smith, Peter H. *Labyrinths of Power: Political Recruitment in Twentieth-Century Mexico.* Princeton, N.J.: Princeton University Press, 1979.

Smith, Peter H. "La política dentro de la Revolución: El Congreso Constituyente de 1916–1917." *Historia Mexicana* 22, 3 (January–March 1973): 363–95.

Spalding, Hobart A., Jr. *Organized Labor in Latin America*. New York: Harper and Row, 1977.

Spalding, Rose J. "State Power and Its Limits: Corporatism in Mexico." *Comparative Political Studies* 14, 2 (July 1981): 139–61.

Stevens, Evelyn. "The Mexican Presidential Succession." *Journal of Interamerican Studies and World Affairs* 19, 1 (February 1977): 125–26.

Stevens, Evelyn P. *Protest and Response in Mexico*. Cambridge, Mass.: MIT Press, 1974.

Stevens, Evelyn P. "Protest Movement in an Authoritarian Regime: The Mexican Case." *Comparative Politics* 7, 3 (April 1975): 361–82.

Story, Dale. "Entrepreneurs and the State in Mexico: Examining the Authoritarian Thesis." *Technical Papers Series*, no. 30. Austin: Institute of Latin American Studies, University of Texas, 1980.

Story, Dale. "Industrial Elites in Mexico: Political Ideology and Influence." *Journal of Interamerican Studies and World Affairs* 25, 3 (August 1983): 351–76.

Story, Dale. *Industry, the State, and Public Policy in Mexico*. Austin: University of Texas Press, 1986.

Story, Dale. "Policy Cycles in Mexican Presidential Politics." *Latin Amercan Research Review*, forthcoming.

Story, Dale. *Sectoral Clash and Industrialization in Latin America*. Syracuse, N.Y.: Maxwell School of Citizenship and Public Affairs, 1981.

Story, Dale. "Trade Politics in the Third World: A Case Study of the Mexican GATT Decision." *International Organization* 36, 4 (Autumn 1982): 767–94.

Tello Macías, Carlos. *La política económica en México 1970–1976*. Mexico: Editorial Siglo Veintiuno, 1979.

U.S. Department of State. *Country Reports on Human Rights Practices* various years. Report Submitted to the Committee on Foreign Affairs, U.S. House of Representatives and to the Committee on Foreign Relations, U.S. Senate.

U.S. Department of State. "Democracy in Latin America and the Caribbean." Washington: Bureau of Public Affairs, 1984.

Vernon, Raymond. *The Dilemma of Mexico's Development*. Cambridge, Mass.: Harvard University Press, 1963.

Von Sauer, Franz A. *The Alienated "Loyal" Opposition: Mexico's Partido Acción Nacional*. Albuquerque: University of New Mexico Press, 1974.

Walton, John and Sween, Joyce A. "Urbanization, Industrialization and Voting in Mexico: A Longitudinal Analysis of Official and Opposition Party Support." *Social Science Quarterly* 52, 3 (December 1971): 721–45.

Wilkie, James W. *The Mexican Revolution: Federal Expenditures and Social Change since 1910*. Berkeley: University of California Press, 1967.

World Bank. *World Development Report* various issues. New York: Oxford University Press.

Index

Abstentionism, 65-66
ACNR (National Revolutionary Civic Action), 94
Agrarian reform, 23, 90-93
Alamazán, Juan Andreu, 99-100
Alemán, Miguel, 5, 29-30, 95-96, 126-27
Authoritarianism, 2, 6-7
Avila Camacho, Manuel, 27-29, 100

Bank nationalizations, 114
Barragán Camacho, Salvador, 89
Buendía, Manuel, 106-7

Cabañas, Lucio, 94
Cabinet, 122, 129-31
Calles, Plutarco Elías, 18-23, 41, 98-100
Camarilla, 119-20
CANACINTRA (National Chamber of Manufacturing Industries), 110-12
Canales Clariond, Fernando, 72-73
Cárdenas, Lázaro, 34, 43, 86, 90-93; and the military, 98-100; nationalizations, 5; as president, 22-26
Carranza, Venustiano, 5, 16-18, 41, 85, 99
Casa del Obrero Mundial, 85
Catholic Church, 19, 27-28, 50, 55, 63-64
CCE (Entrepreneurial Coordinating Council, 35, 113
CCI (Independent Peasant Confederation), 93
Cedillo, Saturnino, 99-100

CEN (National Executive Committee), 77-83, 120
Censorship. *See* Freedom of the press
CFE (Federal Election Commission), 46, 69-70
CGOCM (General Confederation of Workers and Peasants), 24, 86
CGT (General Labor Confederation), 86
Chamber of Deputies: consecutive terms, 21; minimum age, 37; party representation, 4, 32, 39, 53, 64, 72; size, 48; PRI delegation, 120
Chambers Law, 109-10
Chiapas, 101
CIA (Central Intelligence Agency), 107
Científicos, 12
CMHN (Mexican Council of Businessmen), 113
CNC (National Peasant Confederation), 25, 91–93, 120
CNOP (National Confederation of Popular Organizations), 25, 95-97, 120
CONCAMIN (Confederation of Industrial Chambers), 13, 111-13
CONCANACO (National Confederation of Chambers of Commerce), 18, 110-14
Conservatives, 10-11, 13, 41
COPARMEX (Mexican Employers Confederation), 113-14
Corporatism, 5
Corruption, 88-89, 100-103, 106. *See also* Electoral fraud

About the Author

DALE STORY is presently an associate professor of political science at the University of Texas at Arlington and is the author of *Industry, the State, and Public Policy in Mexico* and *Sectoral Clash and Industrialization in Latin America*.

Politics in Latin America:
A Hoover Institution Series
Robert Wesson, Series Editor